STO

D1171622

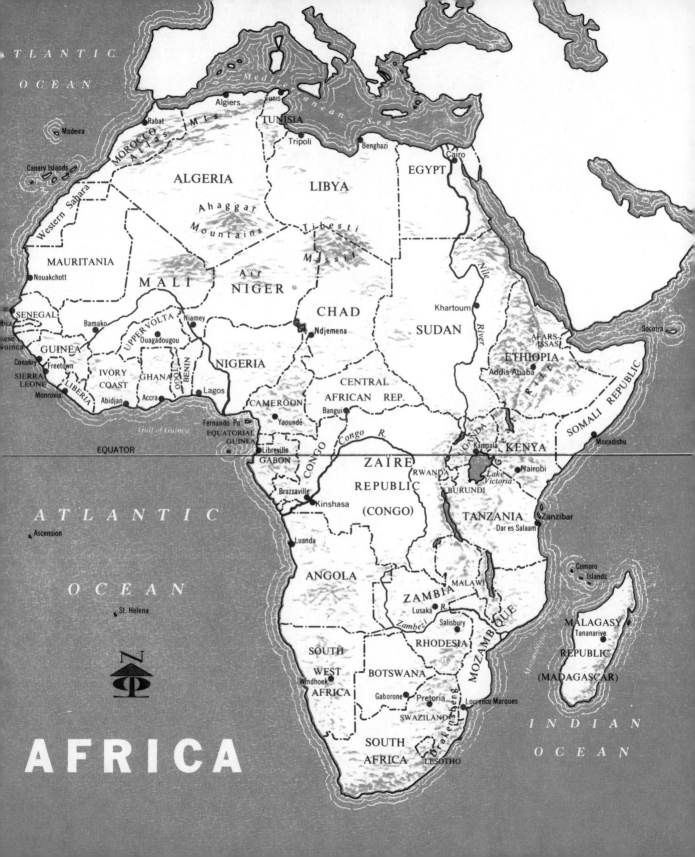

# MALAWI

by Allan Carpenter
and Milan DeLany

Consulting Editor
John Rowe
Department of History
Northwestern University
Evanston, Illinois

CHILDRENS PRESS, CHICAGO

# THE ENCHANTMENT OF AFRICA

Available now: Algeria, Benin, Botswana, Burundi, Cameroon, Central African Republic, Chad, Congo (Brazzaville), Egypt, Equatorial Guinea, Gambia, Gabon, Ghana, Guinea, Ivory Coast, Kenya, Lesotho, Liberia, Libya, Malagasy Republic (Madagascar), Malawi, Mali, Mauritania, Morocco, Niger, Rhodesia, Rwanda, Senegal, Sierra Leone, Sudan, Swaziland, Tanzania, Togo, Tunisia, Uganda, Upper Volta, Zaïre Republic (Congo Kinshasa), Zambia
Planned for the future: Equatorial Guinea, Ethiopia, Nigeria, Somali Republic, South Africa

## BOARD OF ADVISERS, THE PROGRAM OF AFRICAN STUDIES
## NORTHWESTERN UNIVERSITY, EVANSTON, ILLINOIS

Abraham Demoz, Ph.D., Director
Frances A. Leary, Ph. D., Assistant Director
Beth V. Miller, Staff

Ibrahim Abu-Lughod, Ph.D.
Janet Abu-Lughod, Ph.D.
Ethel Albert, Ph.D.
Andrew J. Beattie, Ph.D.
John H. Beckstrom, L.L.M.
Jack Berry, Ph.D.
P.J. Bohannan, D. Phil.
Daniel Britz, M.A.
Dennis Brutus, B.A.
Donald T. Campbell, Ph.D.
Jan Carew, Professor
Remi Clignet, Doctorat de Recherches
Ronald Cohen, Ph.D.
David C. Culver, Ph.D.
George Dalton, Ph.D.
Ralph E. Dolkart, M.D.
Fredric L. DuBow, Ph.D.
Edward B. Espenshade, Ph.D.
Morris Goodman, Ph.D.
Ted R. Gurr, Ph.D.
Errol Harris, D. Litt.
Peter J. Jacobi, M.S.J.
Raymond A. Kliphardt, M.S.

Asmarom Legesse, Ph.D.
Sidney J. Levy, Ph.D.
Judith McAfee, M.L.S.
David Michener, M.S.
Johannes Mlela, M.P.A.
Leon Moses, Ph.D.
Rae Moore Moses, Ph.D.
John F. Ohl, Ph.D.
John N. Paden, Ph.D.
Hans E. Panofsky, M.S.
Arrand Parsons, Ph.D.
Edithe Potter, Ph.D.
John Rowe, Ph.D.
Albert H. Rubenstein, Ph.D.
Robert I. Schneideman, Ph.D.
Walter Scott, Ph.D.
Frank Spalding, J.D.
Richard Spears, Ph.D.
Lindley J. Stiles, Ed.D.
Stuart Struever, Ph.D.
Sterling Stuckey, Ph.D.
Ibrahim Sundiata, Ph.D.
Taddesse Tamrat, Ph.D.
Ralph L. Westfall, Ph.D.
E.H.T. Whitten, Ph.D.
Robert Wilkinson, Ph.D.
Ivor Wilks, Ph.D.
Frank Willett, M.A.

## ACKNOWLEDGMENTS

L.S. Chitsamba, Ambassador, Permanent Mission of the Republic of Malawi to the United Nations, New York, New York; U.S. Information Service, Embassy of the United States of America, Lilongwe; Ministry of Information and Broadcasting, Lilongwe; Alan Taylor, African Studies Program, Indiana University, Bloomington.

Cover Photograph: Woman and child, United Nations
Frontispiece: Rural scene near Zomba, Malawi Information Department

Project Editor: Joan Downing
Assistant Editor: Mary Reidy
Manuscript Editor: Janis Fortman
Map Artist: Eugene Dardeyn

Copyright © 1977. Regensteiner Publishing Enterprises, Inc.
All rights reserved. Printed in the U.S.A.
Published simultaneously in Canada

1 2 3 4 5 6 7 8 9 10 11 12 R 85 84 83 82 81 80 79 78 77

## LIBRARY OF CONGRESS
## CATALOGING IN PUBLICATION DATA

Carpenter, John Allan, 1917-
    Malawi.
    (Enchantment of Africa)

    SUMMARY: Introduces the geography, history, government, economy, animal life, people, and culture of landlocked Malawi.
    1. Malawi—Juvenile literature. [1. Malawi]
I. De Lany, Milan, joint author. II. Title
DT858.C37        968.9′ 7        76-52908
ISBN 0-516-04573-3

# Contents

U. S. 1972744

# A True Story to Set the Scene

## EXPLORING THE ZAMBEZI RIVER

In 1858 the Zambezi Expedition got underway. Led by the famous Dr. David Livingstone, the expedition sailed from England in a ship called the *Pearl*. On board were sections of a smaller boat, the *Ma Robert*. The expedition's destination was the mouth of the Zambezi River, on the coast of East Africa.

Dr. Livingstone had been to that part of Africa before—in fact, just a few years before. He had returned to England to tell of the horrible slave trade he had witnessed in Central Africa. Livingstone traveled through England, asking people to support his fight against slavery. The British government agreed to equip an expedition to look into the matter and to explore the Zambezi River.

A young man named John Kirk was very interested in Livingstone's expedition. Because Kirk was a naturalist and a doctor, he was recommended to Livingstone. Soon the two men became friends, and Livingstone accepted Kirk as his partner in the expedition. John Kirk would serve as the doctor and take notes on the native flora (plants) and fauna (animals).

When the expedition reached the Zambezi, they found a shallow, muddy river. As they traveled along the river, the *Pearl* kept getting stuck. So the group put together *Ma Robert* and continued in the smaller boat.

Bwatoes, *dug-out canoes, are seen on the Shire River and Lake Malawi. This boat, made from tree trunks, can carry up to seven people and last for several years before becoming water logged.*

As they sailed up the muddy river, the group came to the point where the Zambezi is joined by the Shire River. Livingstone and Kirk were attracted by the clear waters of the Shire, so they followed it instead of the muddy Zambezi. They did not know where the river would lead.

They got as far as a village called Chibisa. Then the Shire became too shallow for even the *Ma Robert,* which had been seriously damaged by continually running aground. So they turned back. When they came to the Zambezi River again, they continued up it. All along the way, John Kirk took notes and made drawings.

Beyond Tete (a trading station occupied by the Portuguese), the explorers were aware of a very narrow gorge (called Kebrabassa). Its steep sides rose to twenty-six hundred feet. The rapids in the gorge were so dangerous that the *Ma Robert* would not be able to get through safely. So Livingstone and Kirk left the *Ma Robert* at Tete and proceeded by canoe to the gorge. After bypassing the rapids, they continued on in their canoes. Some distance up the Zambezi, they came to another gorge (the Kariba). But this gorge was not as deep, so they got through it without problems.

Finally the explorers reached the foot of a mighty falls (Victoria Falls). Water poured down over the side of a cliff hundreds of feet high. White foam gurgled and water sprayed into the air as the tremendous volume of water constantly fell into the river. Livingstone and Kirk watched the majestic sight and explored a while, then headed back.

The explorers finally reached the Kebrabassa Gorge. But they almost did not get through alive, for their canoes got caught in the swift currents of the rapids rushing through the dangerous gorge. Dr. Livingstone clung to his canoe, but John Kirk went overboard. Fortunately, Kirk managed to scramble to safety again. But he had lost all of his notes—eight volumes of notes along with more than a hundred drawings of native plants. All his painstaking work and research had gone overboard—and was lost.

The battered *Ma Robert* soon sank, but a new vessel had been sent from England. In it, Livingstone and Kirk sailed up the clear-watered Shire River again as far as they could. Then they continued on foot. They followed the river to its beginning—a large lake (now called Lake Malawi). Around them stood the beautiful Zomba Plateau, with the Mlanje Mountain towering ten thousand feet above them. This beautiful setting the local inhabitants called *Ninyessi,* or "lake of sparkling stars."

*Falls such as these made it difficult for explorers to travel the Shire River.*

UNITED NATIONS

UNITED NATIONS

*The Zomba Plateau is covered with dense forests.*

# The Face of the Land

Malawi is basically a long, narrow valley 520 miles long and only 50 to 100 miles wide. The valley holds Africa's third-largest lake, Lake Malawi (formerly known as Lake Nyasa). From the lake, the land rises to plateaus three thousand to five thousand feet above sea level, with some areas rising to eight thousand feet. The crowning beauty of the highlands is the Zomba Plateau in the south, with

Mount Mlanje towering majestically to ten thousand feet.

Malawi covers an area of 45,747 square miles—about the size of the state of Pennsylvania. Some 20 percent of the area is covered by the surface of Lake Malawi.

## ITS BORDERS

Malawi is a landlocked country; it has no borders on the ocean. Malawi's more densely populated southern region is wedged into the country of Mozambique. The Malawian railway system travels through Mozambique to the seaport of Beira on the Indian Ocean.

Two-thirds of the way up Malawi's eastern side, Mozambique gives way to Tanzania, Malawi's northeastern and northern neighbor. There is a dispute over the border between Tanzania and Malawi. Tanzania claims that the border should go up the middle of Lake Malawi, but Malawi regards its eastern boundary to be on the shoreline of Tanzania.

On the west side is Zambia, and on the southwest is the Tete Province of Mozambique, where the Cabora Bassa Dam is being built. This dam, which will be one of the largest dams in southern Africa, will supply power to Malawi, Rhodesia, Mozambique, and South Africa.

## THE GREAT RIFT VALLEY

Malawi is basically the southern tip of the immense Great Rift Valley, which runs through all of east Africa. A *rift* is a depression or valley formed between two *faults* (fractures in the earth's crust that displace the earth around them, causing one side of the fracture to be lower than the other). Geologists are not sure about the origin of this great rift, but it must have come into being in prehistoric times during a period of tremendous upheavals in the earth's crust.

The Rift Valley—three thousand miles long—has its beginnings in the Dead Sea in Israel. It continues southward through

## MAP KEY

Blantrye, F-4
Bua River, D-3, D-4

Chipoka, E-4

Dwangwa River, D-3, D-4
Dzalanyama Range, E-3

Elephant Marshes, G-5

Great Rift Valley, D-2, D-3

Karonga, B-3

Kasitu River, C-3
Kasungu National Park, D-3
Kirk Range, E-4

Lake Chilwa, F-5
Lake Chuita, E-5
Lake Malombe, E-5
Lengwe National Park, G-4
Lilongwe, E-3
Lilongwe Plain, E-3
Lilongwe River, E-3, E-4
Limbe, F-4
Lintipe, E-4
Lintipe River, E-4

Livingstonia, B-4
Lufira River, A-3, A-4

Mangoche (Fort Johnston), E-5
Mlanje Mountains, G-6
Monkey Bay, E-4
Mount Dedza, E-4
Mzuzu, C-4

Nkota Kota, D-4
North Rukuru River, B-3
Nyika National Park, B-3

Nyika Plateau, B-3

Phalombe Plain, F-5

Rumpi, B-3

Shire River, G-5, G-4, F-4, F-5
South Rukuru River, C-3, B-3, B-4

Tengani, F-5

Vipya Plateau, C-3

Zomba, F-5
Zomba Plateau, F-5
Zomba Range, F-4

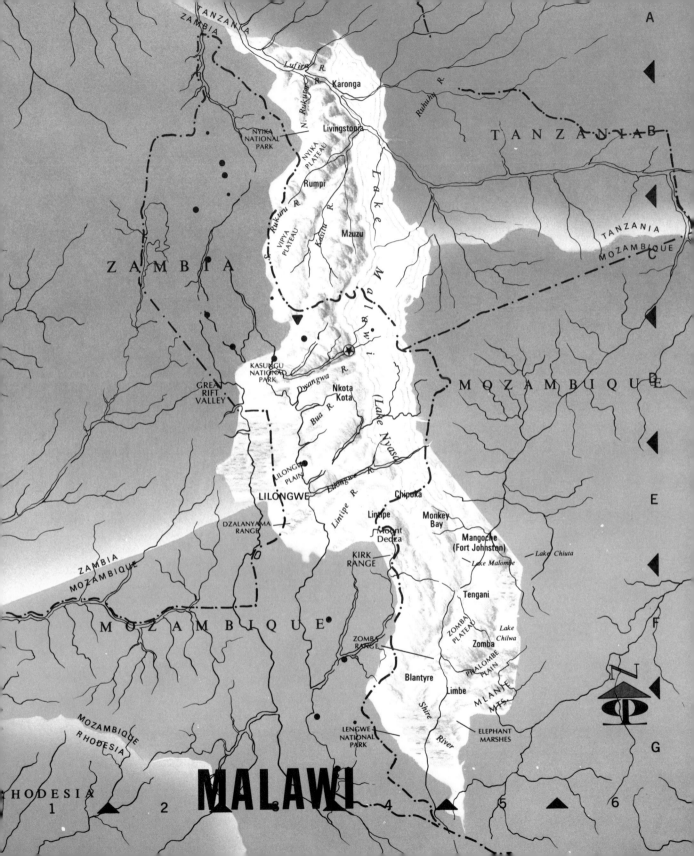

MALAWI INFORMATION DEPARTMENT

*A train stopped at the Limbe railway station, the headquarters of the Malawi railways.*

the Red Sea and across through the Ethiopian mountain ranges. Then it runs through East Africa, cradling all the lakes in its trough, including Lake Tanganyika, which is 450 miles long. Then as the Rift Valley emerges from Tanzania in the south, it becomes the backbone of the whole country of Malawi and culminates there in a burst of scenic splendor.

Lake Malawi is cradled in the Great Rift. Although its surface appears at an altitude of some 1,500 feet above sea level, the greatest depth of the lake is 2,300 feet. In these spots, the Rift Valley

MALAWI INFORMATION DEPARTMENT

*Lake Malawi is the third largest lake in Africa.*

is very deep indeed, going down to 750 feet *below* sea level.

At the southern tip of the lake exits Malawi's main river, the Shire. This river flows south into the great Zambezi River, and together they flow out into the Indian Ocean. Where these rivers meet is the end of the Great Rift Valley.

## LOWLANDS

The Shire Valley, with its fertile lowlands, lies between the Kirk and Zomba ranges. The Shire winds it way past many sugarcane and cotton fields. Sugarcane and cotton are the main crops of this two-hundred-mile-long valley. The altitude of the lower Shire is only about three hundred feet. In the extreme south of the valley is a marshland called the Elephant Marshes. It is rather hot and humid in the Shire Valley, with temperatures rising in some places to 115 degrees Fahrenheit.

## HIGHLANDS

Except for the valley of the Shire River, most of the land in Malawi rises to isolated ranges and plateaus. High savanna regions (areas of coarse grass and trees) of two to three thousand feet stretch between the plateaus. There are lowlands along the western coast of Lake Malawi, but generally these are not very wide, and the land rises quickly into higher regions.

In Malawi's Northern Region, the first high plateau is the Nyika. Much of the Nyika Plateau is now a national park open to visitors year round. Most of the park lies at an altitude of seven thousand feet and consists of rolling grassland with deep valleys in between. Here and there are patches of evergreen forests.

A little farther south, but still in the Northern Region, is the Vipya Plateau. Its highest points are only just over six thousand feet. A main road travels through this hilly plateau area for sixty miles, so the beauties of this region can be enjoyed by many. The Vipya Plateau has a variety of game, especially buck. The many wild flowers color the hills with red, yellow, purple, and white, especially between August and November, when the flowers are at their best.

Since there is no game park in the Vipya Plateau, special agricultural products can be grown there. At present, experiments are being made with planting tung-oil trees in the northern fringes of the plateau. The oil of the seeds of the tung-oil tree, which originally came from China, is used for the production of varnishes and linoleum. There are also pine forests in the Vipya for the production of lumber.

The Central Region has moderately hilly areas, but not nearly as hilly as the Northern and Southern regions. A small range of hills called the Dzalanyama Range lies on the western border between Malawi and Mozambique. South, and still on the border, is a small but very attractive mountainous region centering around Mount Dedza, 7,415 feet. Farther along the Mozambique border is the long

MALAWI INFORMATION DEPARTMENT

*The warm climate in the Shire River valley is good for growing cotton.*

Kirk Range, named after the early Scottish explorer, John Kirk.

Malawi's Southern Region has had the most development. The largest commercial city in the country—Blantyre—is located in this region. Contrasting against the lowlands of the Shire Valley, the Zomba Plateau stands out for its beauty. Averaging seven thousand feet high, the Zomba Plateau attracted the earliest settlers because of its bracing climate, clear mountain streams, and breathtaking panoramic views.

In the extreme southeastern corner of Malawi is one of the most spectacular mountain regions, with Mount Mlanje towering around ten thousand feet. The attractive Mlanje cedar is native to this area. This beautiful region is a favorite attraction for tourists and mountain climbers.

## LAKES AND COASTLINES

Because Malawi is a landlocked country, it has no seacoast. But Lake Malawi, which runs the length of the country, makes up for the lack of a seacoast. This enormous freshwater inland sea, with its sparkling blue waters, measures more than nine thousand square miles. Many sandy beaches and resorts stretch along Lake Malawi. All the resorts are kept clean and free from dangerous animals such as crocodiles. Some 220 species of fish, large and small, provide a real paradise for the fisherman. Boating, yachting, and water skiing are popular sports on this huge lake. The many ornamental trees, both indigenous (native) and imported, give a restful and charming setting to the resort area, and the climate is pleasant.

There are two smaller lakes in the Southern Region. Lake Malombe lies on the Shire River just a few miles south of Lake Malawi, and Lake Chilwa lies just east of Zomba, the old capital city, touching the Mozambique border. There are not as many varieties of fish in the smaller lakes as in Lake Malawi. But there are still enough fish to attract fishing industries and resorts when the area is more fully developed. Waterfowl abound around these two lakes.

Another small lake is Lake Chiuta, located in the east, on the border with Mozambique. The lake is cut in half by the boundary line running north to south. The lake is about the size of Lake Malombe and has swamps along the edges.

*Traders gather on the shore of Lake Chilwa to buy fish.*

UNITED NATIONS

# RIVERS

Lake Malawi gets its water supply from the numerous rivers flowing into it from the surrounding highlands and plateaus. Most of these rivers supply good clear water, and many have an abundance of fish. Some of these rivers are longer than one might expect, considering the narrowness of the country, but the rivers wind through the hills for long distances before reaching the lake.

In the Northern Region is the Lufira River and a somewhat longer river, the North Rukuru. These rivers run north of the Nyika Plateau. The North Rukuru joins Lake Malawi near the coastal town of Karonga. Between the Nyika and Vipya plateaus is one of the longest rivers in Malawi—the South Rukuru. It starts in the southern end of the Vipya Range and flows north quite a distance before it is joined by another river from the Nyika Plateau, the Rumpi River, before it empties into Lake Malawi. A tributary from the northern Vipya Range, the Kasitu River, joins the South Rukuru near the rather important town of Rumpi. All these rivers flow from the west. On the eastern side, only one river, the Ruhuhu, flows into the lake.

The Central Region has two fairly long rivers, the Dwangwa and the Rusa, which empty into the lake north of Nkota Kota, a resort and fishing town. Farther south, the fairly long Lilongwe River (with its tributary the Lintipe) flows through the area of the capital, Lilongwe. All these rivers flow east from the higher savanna and hilly regions.

There is only one important river in the Southern Region—the great Shire River. This river flows *out* of the lake, while all the other rivers flow *into* the lake. The Shire River flows out of Lake Malawi in the Fort Johnston area before merging into a smaller lake—Lake Malombe. It flows out of this lake for some 250 miles before it joins the mighty Zambezi River in the south and with it flows into the Indian Ocean by way of Mozambique. A few tributaries rise in the Kirk Range and join the Shire from the west.

# REGIONAL CLIMATE

There are no deserts or really arid areas in Malawi. The rainfall varies from twenty to sixty-five inches a year in different parts of Malawi. The heaviest rains are in the Northern Region, and the least rain is in the western savanna areas near the Zambia border. Rains are also light in the lowlands along the course of the Shire River.

Generally, Malawi has a very pleasant and mild climate. In the higher altitudes around Lilongwe, the temperature ranges from sixty to seventy-five degrees throughout the year. It is warmer in the lowlands, where the temperature usually ranges from sixty-eight to eighty degrees. High in the plateaus and mountains, it is much cooler, with a touch of frost during the night in the Nyika and the Mlanje Mountains.

MALAWI INFORMATION DEPARTMENT

*Ena has learned to pound the corn used for their main dish, nsima.*

# Five Children of Malawi

## ENA FROM TENGANI

The appearance of the new day's sun over the village of Tengani was noted by the usual stirrings of early morning. Dust rose in the air from the herds of cows and goats being driven by young boys from corrals in the village to outlying grassy areas. Roosters crowed and chickens flapped and clucked as people began to emerge from the dark interior of their huts and sit in the warm sun. Greetings of *bondia* were heard as the people began to move about and see their neighbors.

Ena, sleeping with her younger sister in the *bwalo* (young girl's hut) near her parents' hut, was awakened by these familiar sounds. She rose happily to start the day. This was a special time in her life, for she was over twelve years old and had recently become a *namwali* (a young

woman) in the eyes of her village. Because of this, many new things were happening to her. Each day now, she was instructed by the *mphungu,* a woman chosen by the

families to teach the adolescent girls. The teacher told the girls how to care for their appearance, how to practice good hygiene, how to behave and relate as young women, especially how to show respect for their elders, and how to be good wives and homemakers for their future husbands.

In two months, the great *china mwali* (initiation ceremony) would be celebrated for Ena and her peers. This was a very special event, held only two times a year for all those girls who were ready for marriage. During its three days, they would learn many new things known only to the initiated woman. There would be many instructions, much dancing, and tests of character and skills. To end the festivities, all those present would share in a great feast with fried chicken, sugared tea, bread, and other special foods.

Ena thought about these coming events as she absentmindedly wrapped her *nsaru* (long skirt) around her slender body. Enough daydreaming! She picked up the battered tin water can, mounted it on her head, and began the half mile walk to the well.

Nearing the well-worn path to the water hole near a huge baobab tree, she heard Mattiasi playing his *ulimba,* an instrument similar to a xylophone. He had been taught how to make it and play it by a man who lived across the river in the country of Mozambique. In the evenings when the daily work is done, Ena and her friends often visit Mattiasi and dance in circles to the ulimba's delicate music.

As she approached the well, Ena saw some boys on their way to the small village school. She wished that she could write things on the ground as she often saw the schoolchildren do. But Ena knew that school fees were too high for her parents and other average villagers to afford. Most of the villagers were very poor and grew only enough food to feed their family. They had little left over to sell to the government or at the market. If money was available for education, boys were given the first chance. Besides, the girls had to help their mothers gather the daily food, pound the corn or millet for their main dish (called *nsima*), cut firewood, and care for the younger children. Ena had no time to go to school.

Reaching the well, she stood in line as women pumped water one by one. After her turn, she lifted the now-heavy two-gallon tin can back on her head and returned home.

The water was used by all the family to drink, wash their faces, and rinse their mouths. The rest was put into an earthen pot mounted on three stones with firewood in between. This would be boiled and used to cook the starchy mush, nsima, for the noon meal.

As she prepared the firewood, Ena chewed her breakfast, *nkute,* the hardened cake of nsima left over from the previous night's supper. And once again, her mind wandered as she thought of Chulu, her husband-to-be. He was of the Amanganja clan, the special clan to which all area chiefs belong. Ena was a member of the Asena clan.

Chulu was busy building their new home in his village of Mkanga. Already the hardened mud was packed four feet high around the frame wall made of thick tree branches or slender trunks. Chulu had already saved up the bride wealth money which he must give to Ena's parents and the mphungu. He had worked in the small village store for several years after going to school for eight years. Also he had grown cotton, which he sold to the government's Farmers Marketing Board (FMB). Suddenly she recalled that the FMB was sponsoring a dance that night! She smiled at the thought of seeing Chulu there.

The morning passed quickly for Ena as one task after another was finished for the day. In the late afternoon, she decided to go to the Shire riverbank, where all the women gathered to wash their clothes, cooking utensils, themselves, and their babies. Because of the dance that evening, and because she was a namwali, Ena would give special care to her bath and clothes.

When she reached the riverbank, the girls were screaming and splashing in the water, enjoying its coolness after the heat and dust of the village. Ena quickly removed her nsaru and dove in after them. Once in the water, she hated to leave it. After soaping and scrubbing herself with a special stone and taking a final rinse, she climbed the bank to sun dry herself. Like most of the older girls, she had a string of beads called *danda* around her hips.

One of her friends noticed the fine tat-too marks on her abdomen which had recently been put on. There were symbols of a tree and a bird. One of the village women was skilled in cutting these markings on the skin with a razor. Although it was painful, it soon healed and left rather attractive beauty marks. Now Ena wrapped her nsaru around herself, the small hip scarf called *mpango* round her hips, and tied on her *duku*, a small head scarf.

She now felt good, revived by the swim and wearing clean clothes. Ena looked forward to the evening meal and the dance—and to seeing Chulu.

## SINOS OF LINTIPE

The men of the village were clustered in a small circle, talking angrily. Once again this year, as their crops had begun to ripen in the fields, the baboons had come at night to steal the villagers' corn. Now each man would have to keep a nightly vigil from the wood and reed watchtower that each man built on his land.

Sinos, whose years brought him to the edge of manhood, approached the group and slid into a spot near his father so he could catch all the words. As he listened to his father boast to the crowd of his long hours of watch in the black African night, with only a small fire in the tower, Sinos felt a twinge of pride at his father's courage. But Sinos also felt a sense of annoyance. The village men had been going through this ritual for many years, always accompanied by complaints, always with a shake of their heads that they must do it differently this year.

Sinos had wanted to stir them out of their traditional patterns of acting and ways of thinking, for he felt that surely there were alternatives. Why couldn't all the men join together in a cooperative? They could make traps, or put their money together to buy some firearms and take turns guarding all the fields. But no, he couldn't even suggest these things. They were his elders and were not to be questioned by one as young as he. It would be an embarrassment to his father if he should speak out in the crowd and give his opinion. He must bide his time.

Sinos raised his two fists to shoulder level, clenched, and shook them as a sign that he was departing. One or two in the crowd, including his father, recognized his departure.

Walking back to his home, Sinos's thoughts were a bit sullen. He pulled his handmade slingshot from the back pocket of his shorts and aimed at a small bird in a guava tree. Sinos often felt this tension within himself. He had learned from his parents and circle of relatives the roles and rules of his people. The causes of all the natural events he saw around him each day had been explained, and he had been told what he must do to make good things happen and how to prevent evil. He had been taught the religious acts he must perform to bring the rains, steps he must take to prevent various illnesses, and objects he must keep in his dwelling to protect himself and his family.

Yet Sinos was often confused, for some of the things he learned at the village school suggested other explanations. The new medical assistant who had come to his village and ran a dispensary had become another source of information. Sinos liked to look at all the medicine bottles and instruments that were in the one-room building the government had built. The medical assistant had also taken a liking to Sinos and told him about the common illnesses that were always present in the village and how they could be prevented or cured.

These explanations and cures were quite different from those of his parents. His mother made her own *mankhwala,* or medicine, from leaves and bark or else tied a piece of twine around the painful area. What should he think? What should he believe? It was all very confusing to Sinos, even though everyone said he was a very clever boy.

As Sinos approached his home, another thought struck him. He looked at his house and the few possessions his family had —their sleeping mats, garden hoes, cooking pots, and a few utensils. He said to himself: "My parents are content, for we manage to survive by growing our own food and selling the meager excess at the market. But I have seen sights around town of which my parents have only heard. There are other villages, bigger ones, where many men own bicycles and sewing machines, by which they earn a living. There are even some who own radios, and people gather to listen to the

UNITED NATIONS

*This environmental health worker, like the medical assistant Sinos talks to, gives lectures to mothers on nutritious diets for their babies.*

Malawi Broadcasting Company, which broadcasts from faraway Blantyre."

Sinos had once been to Lilongwe, one of the main towns in that part of the country. What sights he had seen there! Two- and three-story buildings, automobiles, stores with hundreds of things to look at and desire. In that great town were many strange-looking people, too: Malawians from other ethnic groups (evident by their different style of dress), Indians, and white people with different colors of hair.

Sinos realized that the world was very much larger than that of Lintipe . . . but how could he explain this to his father? Recently the two of them were talking about the planting they would have to begin next season. Sinos suggested that they put some of their money toward fertilizer. They could expect to have a better yield if they did so. His father, however, was skeptical of the new ideas that his son learned in his agriculture class. He had always done without fertilizer and gotten a good harvest. Why change?

This was the question that haunted Sinos, for he found himself on the cutting edge of change that was taking place all over Malawi. He belonged to the younger generation who had been to school, who had traveled outside their own villages and seen other ways.

Sinos decided that he would wait, learning more and more until he was the father of his own home and able to make his own decisions. Then he would use fertilizer, grow more crops, earn more money, and buy more things. Yes, he would just wait for his time to arrive.

## ELASI FROM BLANTYRE

Elasi could hardly believe his eyes. Was this really Blantyre, his own home? Everywhere he looked, he saw flags, balloons, and brightly colored displays. Each day the Republic Day preparations had become more and more festive, but today it seemed that every shop on Victoria Avenue had a picture of His Ex-

*Many new houses, like this one, have been built in Blantyre.*

UNITED NATIONS

cellency the President in its window, surrounded by the black, red, and green of the Malawi flag. Elasi had learned in school what these colors symbolized: black for the skin of the men who love "Mai Malawi" ("Mother Malawi"), red for the color of the good red earth of their land, and green for the lush vegetation surrounding them and giving them life. Never before had the sight of these colors given Elasi such a feeling of excitement and pride.

There had been other Republic Day celebrations, of course, but Elasi had never seen one in Blantyre. His family had moved to Blantyre from Zomba only a few months previously. Before that they had lived in Lilongwe, which was now the new capital. But Elasi had been younger then, and even last year's celebrations seemed very long ago. Yes, it was very exciting to be in Blantyre, the busiest urban area in Malawi, for July 6—Republic Day.

Elasi's father, a government clerk who now worked in the passport office in Blantyre, had been born near Lilongwe. Elasi's mother came from a small village in the same beautiful region of the country. They would often tell Elasi stories of life in the small peaceful Chewa villages of their childhood. And Elasi would listen wide-eyed to the tales of a life that he himself would probably never know.

His own life had begun in the hospital near Lilongwe. Except for the yearly visits to his mother's village during the time after the heavy rains, Elasi had always lived in the city. Although it was true that he eagerly looked forward to those times spent at his grandmother's knee near a warm fire on a starry African night, even the excitement of her magical stories about Mr. Rabbit and his adventures did not seem to compare with the present excitement. Everywhere one looked, Blantyre and its "twin sister city" of Limbe were plainly decked out for a real celebration.

Since it was also a school holiday, there were many young people among the quickly gathering crowd on the road to Kamuzu Stadium. Elasi strained his neck to see if any of his friends were in sight. He, Karim, James, and Eric were almost inseparable. They were all Standard Five (fifth grade) students and in the same class at school. The day before, they had agreed to meet somewhere near the great clock in town. The sun was still low in the sky, so Elasi knew that he was not late. But where were they?

*"Moni!!"* A chorus of greeting sounded suddenly behind him. Elasi gave a start and turned quickly to see his three grinning friends.

"You forgot to look behind you!" Eric said. "We've been behind you for a full five minutes!"

Elasi laughed, and the four friends started off single file along the busy road to the stadium. Elasi couldn't remember ever having seen so much traffic—and all of it going in the same direction! The four friends were indeed a happy sight, and many of the passing motorists could not help but notice this small "international" group with a smiling nod.

MALAWI INFORMATION DEPARTMENT

*Above: Traditional dancers perform at Kamuzu Stadium on Republic Day. Below: Members of the League of Women escort President Banda into Kamuzu Stadium during the celebration.*

MALAWI INFORMATION DEPARTMENT

In the lead was James, a boy from the Tumbuka people in the north. He had a brightly colored feather stuck in his smart little straw hat. Elasi remembered when James had first come to Blantyre. He had been very shy on his first day in school, for James's first language was neither Chichewa nor English. He had learned to read first in Chi-Tumbuka, the language of the people from the Northern Region, from which his family had come. But Elasi remembered what had happened when the time for physical education had come that day in school. How quickly the shyness had disappeared when James scored point after point for his admiring soccer teammates. After that game, he had never been shy about speaking out in Chichewa, the national language. With the help of his new friends, some of whom even started to pick up some words from his Chi-Tumbuka dialect, James's shyness gradually disappeared. "And now, he is leading the parade!" thought Elasi.

After James came Eric, his blond hair sporting a flamboyant blossom that James had given him. Eric was the son of missionaries who were now stationed in Blantyre. He had been born in London, but "Mai Malawi" was as much home to him as it was to his other friends. It was here that he had learned many important things. He had learned how impossible it is to catch the quick little lizards that sun themselves on the rocks. He had learned how to be very careful of anything that grows, to respect a snake, and to fear the biting safari ant. But most important, he had learned what it is to be a friend and how important it is to keep a promise.

Eric's two little sisters had even been born here in Malawi, right across the street in the Queen's Hospital. But Elasi hardly recognized the Queen's today, for the entrance had a huge decorated arch of animals and flags. The boys were very close to the stadium now, and Elasi could see the booths that had been set up nearby.

Behind Eric was Karim, an Indian whose father owned a shop near the Blantyre open market. Almost daily the other boys would walk Karim home and stop by the market to bargain with their few *tambalas* (pennies) for a succulent mango or guava. Then they would arrive at Karim's with very hungry looks on their faces. Sometimes Karim's mother would be making curry or hot pickle, and it was important to look hungry if one wanted to be able to taste some of her delicious Indian cooking.

Elasi could now make out Independence Arch farther on, where vibrant colored flowers marked the date and where the flag flew proudly in the gentle wind. The flags marking the road showed the way into the stadium, and the boys hurried, anxious to get good places.

Soon the festivities would begin. There would be colorful dancing groups from many of the schools, and adult dancers in costume would perform for the president. The drill teams would display their precision, and marching bands would fill the air with music. The most exciting part would be the appearance of the home guard. Elasi knew that the sight of the leopard skins worn by the guard along with their smart uniforms would make his heart skip a beat.

The short hike and the excitement had made the boys very hungry. They began to look around at all the little stalls that had been set up for tasty snacks. Suddenly they all recognized a familiar scent in the air—freshly roasted young corn! They quickly dug into their pockets for coins and then sat down to eat. The sweet juice of the corn refreshed them, and the sound of their laughter mingled with the noise of the crowd.

Suddenly a band began to play, and the boys rushed to a spot where they could see the arrival of His Excellency the President. As the president waved his greetings to the crowds, Elasi was sure that for just a moment he smiled right in the direction of the four young boys. "No, I couldn't have imagined that," thought Elasi. "He looked right at us, and he smiled. I know he did . . . but I wonder why?" He looked at James, Eric, and Karim, but they were too busy watching the excitement. "Oh, well," he thought, "it doesn't really matter."

Elasi couldn't remember a happier day than this one with his friends—the day when the black, red, and green of the flag unfurled in the breeze high over their heads. And years later, he would think back and remember how he thought that the president had looked at the four of

them and smiled. And sometimes he would think that maybe it really had happened.

## ESNATI OF THE PHALOMBE PLAIN

The Southern Region of Malawi boasts the awesome presence of the Mlanje Mountain, sheer cliffs of rock and vegetation that rise ten thousand feet above the flat stretch of the Phalombe Plain. Scattered one by one, or in clusters, the square mud-and-grass huts of the Alomwe people speckle the green plain with life.

Since most of the population are Christians, on Sunday morning they can be seen filing along field paths or the main dirt road toward the weathered brick church. Some of the churches use drums and rattles made from long seed pods to support the singing of the congregation and choir. Few of the church buildings have pews; most offer the church-goer simply a cement or mud floor for sitting on. Since few families own chairs, the people are accustomed to sitting or squatting on the ground. The children crawl around the church floor and sit on anyone's lap, while the infants nurse from their mother's breast.

Twelve-year-old Esnati sat on the right side of the church hall with her mother and the other women, but her attention often wandered to the left side, where her two younger brothers sat among the men.

*A cluster of houses, some with thatched roofs and some with metal roofs. Many of these houses have a shaded area in front where the family can sit and relax and have their meals.*

In many ways, throughout each day, Esnati experienced this separation. At mealtime, during bathing, and during work duties, men and women usually maintain their distance from each other.

It is the custom of Esnati's mother to walk to the market which is located on the Phalombe road. She usually goes there after church to buy something special for the noon meal. This day, Esnati and her brothers begged their mother to buy them a stalk of raw sugarcane to chew or a juicy mango fruit. But they were not disappointed when their mother said no, for they knew that she had saved up for some expensive rice.

Walking back to their hut, Esnati carried one of the small baskets of vegetables on her head. She delicately stepped her way along the path, balancing her basket without letting it slip off. She had little trouble, for she had been doing this for years, ever since she was a little girl.

African girls begin learning the skills of their mothers while still quite young. Much of their time is spent with their mother and following her example: learning to cook, caring for younger children in the family, and cultivating the family garden.

Once back at their home, while Esnati helped her mother prepare the meal and attend to other family needs, she watched her brothers amuse themselves. The boys climbed trees to pick fruit, teased the chickens and dogs, and made toys out of bamboo reeds.

Within the next year or so, Esnati would take part in ceremonies initiating her to adulthood. She looked forward to that time in her life. But right now she was thinking of when she had been young. She remembered the foot-high mortar and pestle carved from a tree trunk that she had had—a child-size model of the implements owned by every adult woman. She thought of herself imitating her mother's daily example, pounding a handful of corn kernels into flour.

Esnati looked down and laughed. Here she was, no longer a child, pounding corn kernels into flour. The flour would be cooked in water until very thick and doughy. The result would be nsima, the main food of each meal. Esnati had spent many hours as a child, practicing how to prepare this staple. As she got older, she had learned some of the many rhythmic "pounding songs" sung by the village women as they skillfully heave the heavy five-foot-long pestle in and out of the wooden mortar.

When the meal was ready, Esnati called her brothers. When they all reached the veranda, their mother was already setting out the bowls of food. Esnati and her brothers rinsed their hands in the pan of water nearby. Her father and brothers sat on the veranda and ate with relish each handful of rice and vegetables. Once the men were settled with their food, Esnati and her mother entered the small cooking area attached to the hut and also began eating.

In the midst of their meal, a low mur-

mur of distant voices grew into a confusion of shouts and sounds as a small crowd of people ran past their compound. Esnati's father called out to the group and was told that two rabid hyenas had attacked several people in the next village. The group was going to ask for help from the small mission hospital down the road. Since it was the dry season in Malawi, many animals such as baboons, hyenas, and wild cats often came down from the mountains to the plain in search of food and water. Esnati knew that hyenas are scavengers, eating only dead flesh, but a rabid animal would bite other creatures. Thus, it was feared by the villagers.

Before long, Esnati saw the battered truck used as a hospital ambulance coming along the dirt road filled with a crowd of villagers, now directing the way back to the place where the injured people waited. But Esnati knew that the truck would probably not be able to drive up to the hut with the injured people. Once the undergrowth became too dense for the truck to get through, it would stop. The people would then carry the injured on bamboo stretchers to the truck.

Later in the day, Esnati and her family watched the hospital ambulance return, jogging over the bumpy road. All that day, the family talked about the incident.

That night Esnati tossed restlessly on her reed sleeping mat. Sleep and dreams were mixed with hyenas, ambulances, and crowds. In moments of wakefulness, she listened to the still night and occasionally heard the cry of a hyena.

## AKHIM FROM CHIPOKA

Akhim was fighting sleep, but his eyelids kept on drooping. The gentle lapping of Lake Malawi's waters was like the rhythm of a lullaby, and the warmth from the fire gave him a feeling of security in the cool night air. The men of the village were spending the first of many nights at the shore of the lake, called "fire-flames" by early explorers and immigrants. The men's task was to protect the young corn growing in the marshy lands from the hippopotamuses by chasing the large animals away with torches and shouts. But it was quiet now, and Akhim was nearly asleep.

*Splash! Slurp!* Akhim jumped to his feet. In the amber glow from the fire, he could just make out a huge, dark hulk breaking through the water only fifty yards from shore. Akhim was shaking so much from both excitement and fear that he was glad it was very dark, with no "Drummer in the Moon" to watch him.

Akhim thrust his torch into the fire to light it. Being careful to stay in sight of his father, he then ran with the others into the shallow waters, all the while making great shrieking noises. The poor hippo had time only for one grunting sound before submerging again. The all-clear signal was given, and the men returned to their places around the fire to dry off and begin their half sleep again. Akhim secretly wondered who had been more frightened, himself or the hungry animal.

Akhim's people were the Yao, a Muslim people for the most part, with a strong

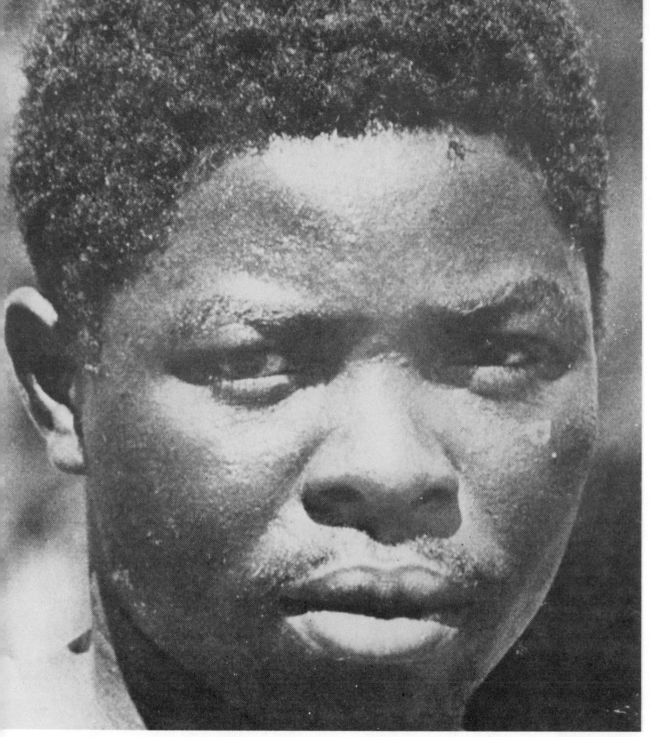

*A villager from Chipoka, near Lake Malawi.*

MALAWI LAND OF PROMISE

community spirit. This task of guarding the crops was one of the men's early duties. This was the first time Akhim had helped guard the crops. It was part of his initiation into manhood. Tonight, in the intervals when it was quiet, Akhim's father was telling him a little about the secret association of the Nyau, to which some of the men in the nearby villages belonged. The Nyau dance, Akhim knew, was very rich in symbolism. Although he did not understand everything his father was telling him, he felt very important to think he was old enough to learn about it. Yes, thirteen years old felt very grown up tonight.

Now and then Akhim thought about the hippo. He knew it was a rather playful animal that meant no harm. But he also knew that the hippo would sometimes have to compete with man for its food. Some days ago, Akhim remembered, when they had been out near the middle of the lake in their dugout canoe, the hippo had been playing nearby in the water. Akhim knew that the hippo's kind of play could become dangerous if the animal came too close to the precious boat and capsized it. The boat, a carved-out trunk of a very special tree, was probably his family's most precious possession. There were only two such boats in his whole village. Without this canoe, how could they ever catch fish, their main food besides corn?

For several years, Akhim had helped with the casting of the nets. First the nets were always spread out on the white sand and examined for breaks. Then they were put into the boat, which the boys would help to launch. When the boys were at least two hundred yards out from the palm-lined shore, they would throw the nets over and carefully spread them out. Then began the long, careful task of gradually moving the nets in toward shore. The young men stayed at the edges of the net, somewhat in the shape of a huge *V*, with the boat at the point of the *V* and the shore at the open ends. The boys, stationed along the arms of the *V*, sometimes actually tried to scare the fish into the net. The closer they came to shore, the quicker they all had to work. Only at the very end, when the nets were gathered in on the sand, would they know how many fish they had caught. Then the whole catch was shared. Akhim smiled when he thought about one especially big catch.

In the quiet, Akhim heard movements on the beach as the baboons came down to snatch the fruit from a tree that looked very much like a mango. But Akhim knew that it was not a mango. He chuckled when he remembered some European visitors who had mistaken the fruit for the juicy orange-colored fruit they loved. How surprised they had been! Akhim guessed that only the baboons liked this fruit. They could have it! It was very tart. The Europeans had stayed that particular day, though, for they wanted to see the beautiful *Ilala II* pass by. She was a large ship, indeed, and Akhim secretly dreamed that one day he might board the ship and cruise the lake, going to see the islands and the northern ports near Karonga.

MALAWI INFORMATION DEPARTMENT

*The* Ilala II, *a passenger vessel on Lake Malawi.*

The movement on the beach had stopped; the baboons had eaten their fill. Akhim knew that in the morning the young boys would take the same fruit and rub it in the sand until all the pulp was removed and the seed could be taken. Using grasses from the water, they would then make a simple whirling toy that went *whoosh! whoosh!* when it was pulled by the strings. When he was younger, he had amused himself with such a toy. He wondered if he was too old for that now.

The long night hours stretched on. The hippo came back only once more, and the men easily scared it away again. Akhim found that in the excitement of the moment, he forgot to be afraid. Instead, he had a feeling of pride in knowing that he was performing an important service with the others in protecting the village's food supply.

A rooster crowed, and sleepy Akhim knew that soon the sky would be gray with the day's first light. Maybe he could still get in a wink . . . but before he knew it, the morning birds were chirping and the huge orange sun was shining right into his eyes. It had just popped up over the mountains on the other side of the great lake. The men had gathered their things and were already walking back toward the huts. There the women would be preparing porridge for breakfast and also warming some bathing water for their husbands, who had spent the long cool night on the wet sand.

Akhim wondered: "When the women slowly let the corn flour slip through their fingers into the hot water, do they remember sometimes how we men spent long nights on the beach standing guard over the young corn?" But this was no time for day dreaming. He rose and started along the beach, passing three small girls who had arrived at the water with clay pots on their heads. When Akhim came near, he heard one of them exclaim that they should hurry back to the village with their filled pots, so that afterward they could quickly return and try to catch the small silvery fish that were darting about in the shallow water. The girl had a small cloth that they would use as a net. Akhim smiled and continued on.

He jumped into the cool water, and his strong, sleek young body sped toward the orange sun. He was awake now, and it was a new day on his beautiful Lake Malawi. As he swam, he thought: "Yes, today I feel just a little older. Maybe after the fishing, I will go visit the family of Ana, the pretty young one who lives near the mill. Maybe." The bright sun reflected in his shining face, and he was smiling.

# Malawi Yesterday

## ARCHAEOLOGICAL FINDS

It is difficult to trace Malawi's early history because few records exist. Although little archaeological excavation has been undertaken in Malawi, sites in nearby Tanzania and Zambia have yielded evidence of prehistoric man that goes back some half million years. At Kalambo Falls at the south end of Lake Tanganyika, several layers have been uncovered going back to the Early Stone Age. In the Broken Hill area of Zambia, a skull was found dating back to the Middle Stone Age. Since these places are near Malawi, it is not surprising that Middle Stone Age tools have been found at the northern edges of Lake Malawi.

It is also known that a group of hunting and gathering people lived along the shores of Lake Malawi long before the birth of Christ. These people were related to the Bushmen of Southern Africa. They lived a peaceful life, fishing in Lake Malawi and hunting in the nearby forests.

In the first centuries A.D., the Malagasy people (who had sailed from Indonesia and settled on the island of Madagascar) were in contact with people on the east coast of Africa. From this contact, East Africans were introduced to the musical instrument known as the xylophone and gained knowledge of banana cultivation. The banana, which originated in Southeast Asia, was a new food to the East Africans. Banana trees could produce enough fruit to support many people. Each tree lasted as long as twenty-five years.

*Bananas are an important source of food for the dense population.*

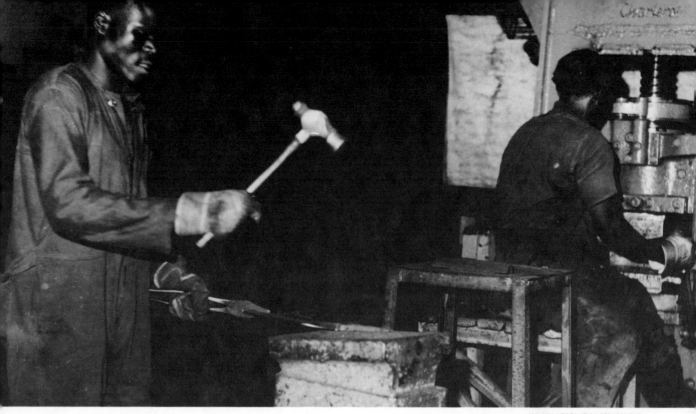

MALAWI INFORMATION DEPARTMENT

*The manufacture of iron tools, like these hoes, is more advanced today in Malawi.*

## NEW KINGDOMS

By the beginning of the third century, new immigrants from the northwest had crossed the Zambezi River and settled in Rhodesia (south of Malawi). They probably settled along Lake Malawi at about the same time. These people (probably Bantu-speaking people) were skilled in making iron tools and weapons.

In the eleventh century, new waves of immigrants began to arrive from the Katanga region of the Congo (Zaïre). They were ancestors of the modern Chewa and Nyanja peoples. These immigrants settled in the area south and west of the lake; this area is still the most densely populated region of Malawi. These people were followed in the 1300s by waves of related Chewa immigrants called the Phili (or Phili-Chewa), who established chiefdoms over the earlier inhabitants.

The earlier settlers were given control over religious matters, because they had already buried their ancestors in the ground. It was thought that these powerful ancestors controlled the fertility of the soil and the crops. The later arrivals (the Phili-Chewa) took charge of politics. Together they established a number of small kingdoms or states, which included most of the peoples of central and southern Malawi—the Chewa, the Nyanja, the Zimba, and the Manganja. It was the desire to control and benefit from long-distance trade that eventually brought these scattered chiefdoms together in a single confederation—the Maravi (or Malawi) empire.

Since the eighth century, Arab and Muslim African traders had built a string of seaports along the southeast African coast. Seeking gold and ivory, these coastal traders moved up the Zambezi River deep into the interior of Africa by 1400. The chiefs of the Lake Malawi region lacked gold, but they were ready to supply ivory in large quantities. Chiefs proclaimed to their people that one tusk from every dead elephant belonged to their chief by right. This "tax" permitted them to collect large numbers of tusks, which they traded to the coastal merchants in return for cloth, beads, and other goods. The ivory was sent downriver and eventually reached India, Arabia, and even as far away as China.

The chiefs used their newly gained wealth from trade to reward loyal followers and increase their influence. In time, one influential chief—whose title was "the Kalonga"—came to dominate all the rest. Thus the Maravi Confederation was born. It prospered on its control of the ivory trade, but its prosperity was soon threatened from an unexpected source.

## THE PORTUGUESE

In 1498 Vasco da Gama sailed around the Cape of Good Hope and discovered the thriving Indian Ocean trade of the East African coastal towns. Other Portuguese soon followed and attempted to take over the trade by seizing the coastland. But their Arab and African merchant rivals struck back by smuggling ivory and gold out through interior rivers and creeks. The Portuguese were desperate to acquire the gold mines of Rhodesia. Driven by "gold fever," they forced their way up the Zambezi and expelled the Muslim merchants.

The Zambezi trading system on which Maravi prosperity depended was destroyed, but the Portuguese seemed incapable of substituting a workable system of their own. Malaria and internal jealousies and rivalries weakened them too much. The Maravi Confederation seemed in danger of breaking up. A powerful ruler (Kalonga) named Muzura responded to the challenge by expelling disloyal chiefs (mainly the Zimba), thereby reuniting his countrymen. Then he sent an army of ten thousand men to open a new trade route directly to the coast.

By the early seventeenth century, Portuguese writers were recording the wealth and greatness of this expanded "Maravi empire." A Portuguese missionary wrote: "The Maravi are very warlike, and are feared—it is a great honor to be a Maravi." Muzura even requested that the Portuguese supply him with special tools so he could construct ships to sail on Lake Malawi, but this was not done. Maravi power began to decline at the end of the seventeenth century, and the confederation drifted apart into its original condition of feuding rival kingdoms. By the 1750s, long-distance trade had been captured by a new and energetic power—the Yao.

## THE SLAVE TRADE

The Yao lived between Lake Malawi and the seacoast in what is now Mozambique. They had become traders in iron and ivory, and they traveled long distances between the coast and the African interior. By the nineteenth century, however, there was a growing demand for a new kind of trade—slaves to work on the sugar plantations on the island of Zanzibar. Coastal Arabs and Swahili traded guns and powder to the Yao, who used these weapons to capture or trade for slaves.

The Yao moved into southern Malawi. By the 1850s, they were clashing with the Nyanja in the Shire Valley itself. Many Yao decided to settle in Malawi, where their descendants are today. Another disruptive group were the Ngoni, a band of warlike people who had been driven from South Africa by the Zulu. In central Malawi, the Tumbuka peoples had cooperated with African traders from Tanzania early in the century. A Tumbuka trading state arose and became prosperous. But it attracted the attention of the Ngoni, who invaded and smashed the Tumbuka state in the 1850s.

Into the turmoil the coastal Arabs and Swahili now advanced, determined to seize slaves for themselves instead of paying the Yao as middlemen. They found the densely populated Shire Valley a fine target for their slave raids. Their guns were more than a match for the Chewa and Nyanja spearmen. It was just at this time that the most famous of all African explorers arrived on the scene.

## DR. LIVINGSTONE

Though he was not the first European to discover Lake Malawi, Dr. David Livingstone was to have the greatest impact on Malawi's history. Livingstone was a great fighter of slavery, especially slavery in Central Africa. Having seen for himself the horrors of slavery there, he spoke to various groups throughout England and Scotland, asking for their help in fighting slavery.

Livingstone's exploratory trip up the Zambezi River with John Kirk was primarily to scout out the situation concerning the slave trade. Seeing that the area of Lake Nyasa (now Lake Malawi) was desirable and not settled by the Portuguese, Livingstone thought it would be a good spot for British settlement. Through Livingstone's persistence and influence with the British government, the interior of Africa was gradually opened up to Christianity, commerce, and British settlement. And ultimately slavery came to an end.

Livingstone died in what is now Zambia in 1873. His death inspired people in England to set up a mission station in the lake country of Central Africa. Thus, in

1875 the first British mission was set up at Cape McLear. In the next few decades, more and more missions were set up throughout the area.

After Christianity came commerce. In 1878 the Livingstonia Central Africa Company (later called the African Lakes Company) was established to open up communications and trade with the local people. But over the years, relations between the company and the missionaries and slavers deteriorated. Thus, in 1883 a British consul was sent to the area.

## MLOZI

At the northern end of Lake Nyasa (now Lake Malawi), lived a group of people called the Ngonde. Unaware of the events taking place to the south, the Ngonde lived peacefully, tending their cattle and crops and hunting for ivory. In 1884 the British opened a trading post at Karonga, only a few miles away from the Ngonde. This post was managed by Monteith Fotheringham.

In 1886 an Arab called Mlozi came to the area to trade. Actually, he wanted to exploit the Ngonde and sell them as slaves. But he disguised his intentions well as he built a stockade at Mpata and persuaded local chiefs to join him. As Fotheringham watched all this, he became suspicious.

Fotheringham's suspicions were well founded, for soon Mlozi and his men attacked the Ngonde and filled the stockades. The slaves were then taken to Kilwa, an Arab port on the Indian Ocean, and from there to the marketplace at Zanzibar.

Furious over what had happened, Fotheringham asked the African Lakes Company for help. For the next eight years, a private war took place between Mlozi and the African Lakes Company.

In the 1880s, the "scramble for Africa" had begun. The European nations agreed to divide the continent into areas of European "influence." The land west of Lake Nyasa would be under British "influence."

A British protectorate was declared over the "Nyasaland districts" (what is now Malawi) in 1891. Sir Harry Johnston was named commissioner of the protectorate.

## END OF THE SLAVE TRADE

Johnston's main goal was to end the slave trade. He knew that he would have to break Mlozi's stronghold in the north before the slave trade would end. But he needed time. So he signed a five-year peace treaty with Mlozi.

Mlozi's power increased in the next five years. During that time, however, Johnston was able to end slave trading in the south and build up a small army. Johnston knew that eventually he would have to fight Mlozi, so he recruited Sikh soldiers from India to serve with his African troops.

In 1895 Mlozi refused to renew the peace treaty; he claimed that the British

MALAWI INFORMATION DEPARTMENT

*Tobacco has been called the "gold" of Malawi.*

had blocked off the slave route to the Indian Ocean. Quickly, Johnston gathered together all his forces and attacked Mlozi's stockade. Finally, the stronghold fell. Mlozi was captured and executed for his crimes. The slave trade in Central Africa was brought to an end, marking a new era in Malawi's history.

## THE NEW ERA

With the defeat of the Arabs, the country was open to European settlers. Many moved into the southern highlands and took lands belonging to the Nyanja and Chewa. These lands were turned into large estates, and the Africans who had once farmed them had to work as laborers for the European owners. By the 1890s, more than one hundred Europeans lived near Zomba and Blantyre on large plantations where cotton, tea, coffee, and tobacco were grown.

Along with the Europeans were other foreigners: Asians who had come to build the railway line, as well as former Sikh soldiers.

## SEEDS OF NATIONALISM

The Africans were discontent with colonial rule. This became evident as early as the end of the nineteenth century. An early spokesman of nationalism was John Chilembwe (a Yao from the south).

After graduating from an American theological college, Chilembwe returned to Nyasaland. He founded a mission station at Magomero and built numerous churches and schools. Many people converted to his new type of African Christianity.

Chilembwe criticized government policy and charged that African laborers working for the European plantations were badly treated. Chilembwe's dream was that Nyasaland would someday be free from white rule.

In 1914 World War I began, and Britain and Germany were enemies. Nyasaland was on the front line with German-occupied Tanganyika. At a battle at Karonga, many Africans died serving as soldiers for the British and Germans. Chilembwe was angry that many Africans had died in a battle that was not their own. So Chilembwe plotted an armed rebellion throughout the country. But the rebellion was put down, and Chilembwe was killed. Chilembwe became Nyasaland's first political martyr.

## THE WORLD WARS

After the battle of Karonga, the British authorities in Nyasaland recruited a local army called the King's African Rifles. When German forces from Tanganyika tried to invade Nyasaland, they were successfully repelled.

Twenty years later, in World War II, the Africans from Nyasaland once again fought with the Allies. Thousands of Africans served in Allied armies in East Africa and Burma, fighting another war that was not theirs.

# Malawi Today

## NATIONALISM REEMERGES

In a referendum in 1922, the British government offered the white settlers of Nyasaland and Northern and Southern Rhodesia the choice between joining the nation of South Africa or continuing their separate existences. None of the territories voted to join South Africa; thus they remained separate. In 1924 Southern Rhodesia became a white self-governing colony; Northern Rhodesia (present-day Zambia) became a protectorate under British rule; and Nyasaland (present-day Malawi) remained a protectorate.

By the end of World War II, Chilembwe's nationalist seeds had taken root, and a new political presence was felt through-out Nyasaland. The people did not want to be ruled by whites; they wanted to govern their own country. These feelings were felt by people all over Nyasaland. Thus, in 1944 the Nyasaland African Congress was founded.

## THE FEDERATION

As the years passed, the British felt that a closer union would benefit its three Central African territories economically and thus lead to greater development. So in 1953 the Federation of Rhodesia and Nyasaland was created. It included Nyasaland and Northern and Southern Rhodesia. All together the Federation occupied an area of 478,243 square miles and had a

*The beautiful area around Mount Mlanje is a favorite attraction for tourists and mountain climbers.*

population of 8.3 million people, 300,000 of whom were Europeans.

Each protectorate retained its own government and its own constitution. In Nyasaland, the governor represented the British government, and the chief executive represented the local government.

The Federation established an overall Federal Assembly of thirty-five European members—fourteen members elected from Southern Rhodesia, eight from Northern Rhodesia, and four from Nyasaland. In addition to these, there were two African members from each territory. Legislative power was divided between the federal and territorial governments. The federal government was responsible for external affairs, defense, communications, and overall development, while the territorial governments controlled African affairs and policy, agriculture, labor, and the mines. A Federal African Affairs Board was established to protect Africans from discriminatory legislation.

But the Federation was unsuccessful in Nyasaland. From the start, African leaders worked against its establishment. They rightly feared that the white settlers of Southern Rhodesia would dominate the Federation and would always look on blacks as inferior. While the British were saying that federation signaled "partnership" between the races, in Southern Rhodesia the whites said it was a "partnership" between horse and rider. The Africans were the horse, and the white settlers were the rider.

Africans sought eventual self-determination, and they knew that this federation would not help them achieve their goal. They regarded the Federation with great suspicion, and events that followed confirmed their suspicions.

For example, when the constitution and electoral bills were published, the African Affairs Board objected to both, but Britain overrode the Board and accepted both the bills. Also, the Africans were dissatisfied that Salisbury (capital of Southern Rhodesia and center of white influence) was chosen to be the capital of the Federation.

In the meantime, the African nationalist movements had grown considerably. In Nyasaland, the nationalist movement was still led by the Nyasaland National Congress. But dynamic young leaders had reorganized it. They began a party newspaper, designed a national flag, and adopted a new slogan for independence— "*Kwacha*," which means "the dawn." But they were searching for a more experienced leader. In 1957 this congress elected as its president Dr. Hastings Kamuzu Banda.

## DR. BANDA

Hastings Kamuzu Banda was born about 1898 and educated in Malawi mission schools. After he finished school he worked as an interpreter in Johannesburg, South Africa. After eight years as an interpreter, he came to the United States in 1925 with the help of the African Methodist Episcopal mission, a black American church. He studied at Wilberforce College

MALAWI INFORMATION DEPARTMENT

*The Life President Dr. Kamuzu Banda.*

in Ohio and graduated from the University of Chicago. Because he was interested in medicine, he enrolled at the Meharry Medical College in Nashville, Tennessee. There he got his first degree in medicine.

Before the outbreak of World War II, Banda went to Great Britain and continued his medical studies in Edinburgh, Scotland. There in 1941 he received his license from Royal College of Physicians, which enabled him to practice medicine in Liverpool. After the war, he settled in London and built up a very successful medical practice.

During this time, Banda was still in-terested in African politics. He kept in touch with African leaders from his homeland. Banda constantly warned against British ideas of federation which would put Nyasaland African labor under Rhodesian settler control. In 1955 Banda left London and settled in Ghana, West Africa, practicing medicine there for three years. As a politician, he took part in the first All-Africa People's Conference held in Accra (Ghana).

This political step taken in Ghana brought Banda ever closer to Nyasaland. During this time, younger Congress leaders had been urging him to turn his experi-

49

ence and educational qualifications toward leadership of the nationalist struggle.

After forty-three years away from his homeland, Banda returned to Nyasaland in July of 1958. The people hailed him as their new "Messiah," and he became a dynamic leader. Immediately Banda took up the fight against the Federation. His opposition was so powerful that in 1959 he was declared a "prohibited immigrant" by both Northern and Southern Rhodesia, arrested, and put in jail.

This step caused much anger and unrest in Malawi. All over Nyasaland, people took to the streets and rioted. The government attempted to restore order by using police and troops. More than fifty Africans were killed. This expression of popular will convinced the British government that the people of Nyasaland could not be forced to continue within the Federation structure. So the British decided to let Nyasaland go its own way.

In April of 1960, Banda was finally released from prison. He assumed leadership of the newly formed Malawi Congress Party. Banda flew to London for talks with leaders of the British government and asked for immediate independence for Nyasaland.

## MALAWI'S INDEPENDENCE

On February 1, 1963, Nyasaland was granted internal self-government and Banda was elected prime minister. That same year, the Federation of Rhodesia and Nyasaland was officially ended. After seventy-three years of British rule, on July 6, 1964, Malawi finally became a sovereign, independent state. Banda became the country's first prime minister. The new nation had a Parliament of fifty elected members and a Cabinet of Ministers headed by Banda.

Independence Day was a great day. Finally, after years of struggling and planning, the nation was free. Throughout the land, the people shouted "*Ufulu! Ufulu!*" ("Freedom! Freedom!") and hoisted the new flag—three horizontal stripes (black, red, and green) with half a rising red sun in the center of the black stripe.

Two years later, on July 6, 1966, Malawi became a republic within the British Commonwealth. The Malawi Congress Party was the only political party permitted in the country. At the party's annual convention, July of 1971, Dr. Banda was unanimously elected "Life President" of the republic. As life president, Banda's full title in the Chichewa national language is Ngwazi Dr. H. Kamuzu Banda.

Malawi followed a significant policy, different from that of many other independent states in Africa. It maintained friendly relations with South Africa and the other southern states, including Portuguese Mozambique. The African independent states severely criticized and censored Dr. Banda for this, but his reply was contained in his opening speech to Parliament in 1971. He stated: "I do what I think is right, in the interests of my people, no matter what anyone thinks, feels, or wants to do . . ."

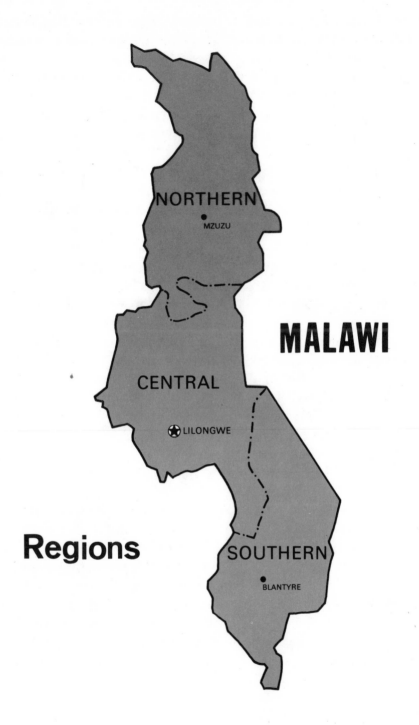

MALAWI

Regions

Banda's friendly relations with South Africa led to the state visit of South Africa's prime minister, Balthazar Johannes Vorster, to Malawi in 1970. This was the first such visit to an independent black state made by a South African leader. South Africa then committed itself to help finance and build Malawi's new capital at Lilongwe.

In return, President Banda visited South Africa in 1971, the first African head of state to do so. He was well received.

Banda's friendly relations with South Africa were clearly dictated by Malawi's poverty. More than 270,000 Malawians had to seek work outside the country, and many of these migrant laborers worked in South African mines. Their wages supported many families at home. In addition, South Africa promised financial aid, which Malawi desperately needed.

Nevertheless, Dr. Banda angrily cut off the flow of labor to South Africa for a time in 1974 when seventy-five workers died in an aircraft chartered by a mine-recruiting company. And Banda managed to maintain secret relations with Frelimo (the Mozambique liberation movement) while appearing to be friendly to the Portuguese colonial government.

## GOVERNMENT

The present constitution provides for a Cabinet consisting of the president and such ministers as may be appointed from time to time by the president. The 1974 Cabinet consisted of fourteen members, including the president. Five of the leading ministries are headed by the president—Ministry of Agriculture, Ministry of Defense, Ministry of External Affairs, Ministry of National Resources, and Ministry of Works and Supplies.

The National Assembly has sixty-three elected members. Since 1964 Malawi has been a one-party state under the Malawi Congress Party. The constitution of this party calls for a six-level political system, from local and district committees at the bottom to the president at the top. In this way, it is hoped that there is full representation for all people, and that the views and wishes of the common citizens are made known.

However, there is little toleration of Africans who refuse to join the party. Jehovah's Witnesses have been severely persecuted for their rejection of party membership on religious grounds. Party officials regard this as treason.

## EDUCATIONAL PROGRAM

Children and students in Malawi appreciate school perhaps more than many children in Western countries, where education is compulsory. Since there are not enough schools in Malawi, less than half of the school-age children attend school. That is why schools are appreciated. Only those who qualify are ac-

*Malawi Congress Party headquarters.*

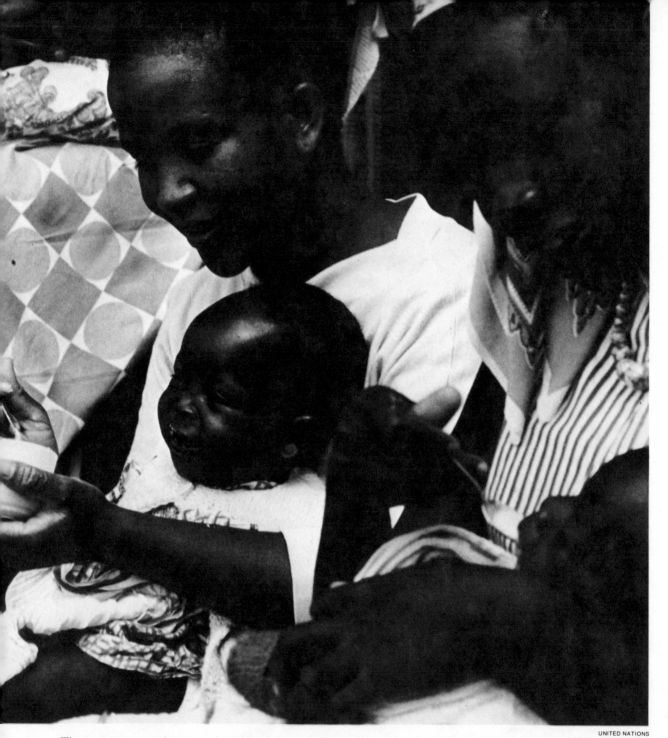

UNITED NATIONS

*These women students are learning home management. After graduation they will help other families improve their living conditions.*

MALAWI INFORMATION DEPARTMENT

*A procession during a graduation ceremony at the University of Malawi.*

cepted into primary school, an eight-year course. Approximately 485,000 children attend primary school, and about 13,500 are enrolled in secondary schools.

In order to expand the school system, better teachers for all grades are needed. There are about fifteen teacher-training colleges throughout Malawi, including a new one in Lilongwe, which accommodates about 540 resident students.

The University of Malawi is located in Zomba. The former capital, Zomba is now the university town and main educational center. This university has branches in other cities, which specialize in fields such as agriculture and technical education.

The educational program is strong and progressive. Although it still has a way to go to satisfy all needs, it is growing considerably from year to year. Good libraries and the Malawi Correspondence College supplement the educational program. Some courses are also offered by radio. Because the hunger for education and knowledge is a constant one, the government has given education top priority.

# Natural Treasures

## ANIMAL LIFE

Compared to other nearby countries such as Kenya and Zaire, Malawi does not enjoy wildlife treasures in huge quantities. Yet all the varieties of game commonly found in neighboring countries can also be found in Malawi. But Malawi's animal life is restricted more to its national parks. Malawi's three main national parks are evenly distributed throughout the country—one in each of the three regions.

Hunting opportunities in Malawi are very limited. Hunting safaris are not organized. Hunting is completely forbidden in the national parks and forest reserves.

**Nyika National Park**    This park is located in the Northern Region and covers about 360 square miles. In this mountainous region, some of the peaks rise to eight thousand feet. The views from these spots are breathtaking. The main lodge and camp, called Chelinda Camp, is located almost in the center of the park.

Great herds of large eland antelope move about freely in this park. These antelope, about the size of cows, prefer higher altitudes rather than low plains. Another very attractive antelope found in this park is the roan. Various other smaller antelopes, such as the bushbuck, impala, hartebeest, and reedbuck, are also found in great numbers in Nyika National Park.

Few large animals, such as the elephant and the rhinoceros, are found in Nyika National Park. These animals prefer the southern part of the country, especially the

*Visitors to Nyika National Park can see a large number of zebras.*

swampy areas of the Shire River. However, there are large numbers of zebras, and in the forested areas of the valleys are different kinds of monkeys. The park is open to visitors year round.

**Kasungu National Park** Covering some eight hundred square miles, this park is the largest of all Malawi's parks and is located in the Central Region. Due to seasonal weather, this park is open to visitors only for eight months, from the beginning of May to the end of December. Here are found a very extensive range of wild animals, including elephants, rhinoceroses, buffalos, and the magnificent kudu and sable antelopes. Zebra, wildebeest, and hartebeest are present in great numbers, along with the many varieties of smaller antelopes. It is natural that wherever there is a variety of game, the predators such as lions and leopards abound as well.

The Lifupa Lodge and Camp is located in the southern half of the park and can accommodate about thirty visitors who want to spend the night.

**Lengwe National Park** Located in the Southern Region, this park is almost at the southern tip of Malawi. It is not very large, only about fifty square miles. But this park is unique. It is the farthest place north in Africa where the very rare and shy nyala antelope is found. The nyala antelope can be seen in this park in fairly large numbers together with other antelopes such as the kudu, bushbuck, impala, hartebeest, and the tiny little duiker. A fairly rare monkey is found in this park—the blue or samango monkey. A herd of buffalo and the ever-present lion and leopard can also be seen here quite often. Big hippopotamuses live in the Shire River.

Like the Kasungu National Park, this park is also open only eight months of the year, from May to December. There is a small camp for visitors—the Lengwe Game Camp—which provides accommodation for only eight people.

### BIRDS

There are many colorful and very attractive birds in Malawi. Various kinds of birds find the country an ideal habitat because of its variety. There are plains, highlands, plateaus, and valleys with patches of forest. Yet only a short distance away is Lake Malawi, which runs parallel to these regions for hundreds of miles.

Because different birds inhabit different kinds of areas, there are hundreds of varieties of birds in Malawi. It is a paradise for an ornithologist (a person who studies birds).

In the wooded higher altitudes are birds with bright plumage and lovely song birds. In the plains are varieties of pigeons and doves, quails, guinea fowl, and the occasional ostrich, as well as eagles, hawks, vultures, and grotesque marabou storks.

The marabou stork associates with the vultures when feasting on the carcass of a dead animal. This bird used to be greatly hunted for commerce because it has very fine fluffy undertail feathers, which were

MALAWI INFORMATION DEPARTMENT

*Roaming through Kasunga National Park are buffalo (above) and elephants (right). The rare nyala antelope (below) can be seen in Lengwe National Park.*

MALAWI INFORMATION DEPARTMENT

MALAWI INFORMATION DEPARTMENT

MALAWI INFORMATION DEPARTMENT

*Fishermen, with their dugout canoes, have just brought in their catch from Lake Chilwa.*

prized for fancy ladies' costumes or hat ornaments.

Another interesting bird is the wise old honey bird. When it sees someone coming, it emits a peculiar call which the people recognize as a "come-on call" to follow the bird to a bee hive. For the bird hopes that the person will then break up the hive and make the honey available.

Lake Malawi attracts many varieties of water birds, ranging from the fish eagle to various ducks and geese, herons, and flamingoes. During certain seasons, some of the geese migrate south all the way from Egypt. The common stork migrates to this area all the way from Europe.

## FISH

Malawi is a small country. But because its heart is Lake Malawi, which runs almost the whole length of the country, fishing is an important industry in Malawi. There are an estimated 220 varieties of fish in the lake itself. Some of these are not found anywhere else in the world. The fish range in size from the six-foot-long catfish, weighing about one hundred pounds, to the tiny whitebaits, which are only three inches long. Fishermen fish in Lake Malawi for catfish, perch, and carp, as well as lake tigerfish and lake salmon.

In the rivers are still other varieties of fish. But what most attracts the fisherman to the rivers are rainbow trout. These have been imported and used to stock the mountain streams. There they have multiplied and now thrive in great numbers.

In the Shire River, in addition to catfish, perch, tilapia, and carp, is an interesting species called the lung fish. Because this fish actually has a true lung, it is able to breathe air almost like an animal. Lung fish often come out of the water; using their fins as legs, they crawl about on the muddy shore.

## THE MLANJE CEDAR

Among the special timber trees in Malawi is the mlanje cedar. This tall indigenous tree grows in forests on the slopes of Mount Mlanje. Mlanje cedars were originally called cedars because to the average person they look like cedar trees. But they are not cedars; they are a rare kind of conifer.

The scent of the mlanje cedars is pleasant and strong, filling the air on Mount Mlanje. The sap that runs through these trees is a thick, yellow, resinous sap of a density unusual in conifers. Even after a mlanje cedar dies, it does not dry up and rot as other trees do. Instead, this special sap preserves the tree so that no insect, worm, or ant will touch it and break it down.

Because these trees are so unusual, their seeds were once collected and exported. Mlanje cedar trees have now been grown successfully in other parts of Africa and the rest of the world.

MALAWI INFORMATION DEPARTMENT

*Special costumes are worn in traditional dances.*

# The People Live in Malawi

## THE PEOPLE

In present-day Malawi, 90 percent of the people are Chewa—descendants of early Bantu groups who settled there before the great Maravi kingdom was established. The Chews are not confined to Malawi but have spread into the northern part of Zambia, into the southern part of Tanzania, and into northern Mozambique. The extent of the Chewa people once gave President Banda the dream to extend Malawi east and west into these areas—even to the Indian Ocean. But such dreams will probably never materialize unless great revolutions take place in those regions. At present, the Chewa set the pace in Malawi. Chichewa, the language of the Chewa, is Malawi's national language.

Other main groups in Malawi are the Ngoni in the east and the Tumbuka in the north. The Nyanja are considered the major group in the south. Since they are very closely related to the Chewa, the two groups can almost be regarded as one. A small number of Yao inhabit the mountainous regions of southeastern Malawi.

As in many other independent African countries, attempts have been made by the government to unify all these peoples through language. Tribalism is discouraged everywhere, and people are encouraged to think of themselves as part of the whole nation rather than part of an ethnic group. Through nationalism, the government hopes to have one united people —Malawians.

Since Malawi was both small and densely populated, it was not colonized as much as were Zambia, Rhodesia, or Kenya. During the British colonial period,

MALAWI LAND OF PROMISE

*A class in Blantyre Secondary School.*

however, some foreigners came to the area. Asians in Malawi now number roughly twelve thousand, and they work mostly as traders or shopkeepers. Europeans in Malawi number around seventy-five hundred. Many of these people were originally in government work or education; some were farmers and others missionaries. Most of these people now help train the Malawians to run the nation and the businesses.

## RELIGION

Most of the people in Malawi are animists. They believe that everything around them—trees, animals, and objects of all kinds—have spirits which must be treated with respect. The spirits of the dead ancestors, too, are revered, and must be honored and cared for in ways dictated by age-old custom.

But for a small state like Malawi, with a rather cohesive population, there are a surprising number of Christians—about one million. The early missionaries represented various Christian churches. Along with religious teaching, the missionaries introduced health and education to Malawi. Nearly all the schools in the country had their start through the churches.

Other important religions in Malawi are

the Eastern religions. The Asians brought with them the Hindu and Sikh faiths, and with the Arabs came Islam.

### THE MEDICAL PROGRAM

Medical work and related services in Malawi are regulated by the Ministry of Health and Community Development. Training the medical staff is one of the main concerns of this ministry. Some medical personnel are trained in Malawi, but many are trained overseas in Great Britain, in the United States, or in South Africa.

The Queen Elizabeth Central Hospital in Blantyre is the largest hospital in Malawi. There are about thirty-eight government hospitals throughout the nation.

In addition to all the common diseases, there are many tropical diseases in Malawi. Malaria is the most prevalent; it is the major cause of death among infants. It is estimated that more than six hundred thousand cases of malaria are treated every year in Malawi.

*A baby being weighed in an under-five clinic.*

MALAWI INFORMATION DEPARTMENT

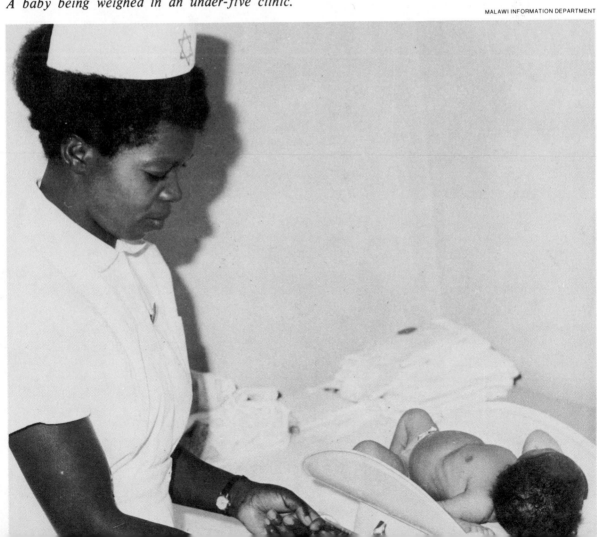

## SPORTS

Many kinds of sports are popular in Malawi. A Department of Sports was set up to organize sports activities and training. Some Malawians take athletic training and special courses overseas. Competitive football games are played against Zambia, Uganda, and Lesotho.

Track and field is very popular in Malawi. National Championship Games are held at the Kamuzu Stadium in Malawi. Two of Malawi's best athletes are Joyce Chanya and Wilfred Mwalwanda. Joyce Chanya has won the 100-meter and 200-meter races as well as the long jump. In a tournament in Cape Town, South Africa, Wilfred Mwalwanda broke not only his own record in javelin throwing, but also the African record.

In recent years, badminton, tennis tournaments, and cycling have become popular in Malawi. A Cycling Association was organized in 1968; since then, there have been many bicycle races in Malawi, usually ten-mile races.

Fishing in Malawi is both a great sport and an industry. Not only do the people fish to make a living, they also fish for fun. This practice was probably started by the British. The Malawi Anglers participate in tournaments as far away as Rhodesia, Angola, and South Africa.

## ART

One way that Malawians express their inner feeling is through art, music, and literature. Traditionally, people told about themselves, their accomplishments, special occasions, or battles through singing and chanting. Others would participate, singing together, and then dancing. Some of the dances would be ritualistic, and special masks would be worn. Like so many other peoples throughout the world, Malawians have historic songs, chants, and dances. Traditional musical instruments were not very elaborate, the basic instrument almost always being the drum. Simple string and twanging instruments or xylophones would also be used.

The government has made an effort to preserve these traditional stories, legends, and songs that were never written down. They were just passed down orally from generation to generation. The government has collected many such songs and legends, recorded them in writing, and stored them in a special museum.

*Young men from the Young Pioneers, a youth group, do exercises at their training base.*

MALAWI INFORMATION DEPARTMENT

# The People Work in Malawi

## FISHING

Malawi's main life and activities center around the great lake that is the heart of the land. Lake Malawi occupies almost one-third of the country's area. Around the lake, fishing has become very important.

Nearly twenty-five thousand people engage in commercial fishing. They not only provide fish for local markets, but also for export to Rhodesia, Zambia, and Mozambique. Of the approximately twenty-five thousand tons of fish caught each year, most of which are cured, dried, or smoked, more than one thousand tons of fish are shipped abroad. Also there is a flourishing trade in live aquarium fish for export.

This unique export brings in about sixty to seventy thousand dollars each year.

## AGRICULTURE

The many people involved in the fishing industry are also involved in agriculture. More than 90 percent of the people in Malawi live on the land, tilling the soil and growing staple foods. Some also grow cash crops, and some also raise cattle and other animals. The people divide most of their time between fishing and agriculture.

Malawi's countryside, with its various altitudes, its valleys and streams and rivers, and its woods and forests, contributes to a successful agricultural program.

Malawians have used their land to the

*Fishermen mending their nets. Some 220 species of fish can be found in Lake Malawi, from the six-foot-long catfish, weighing about one hundred pounds, to the tiny three-inch-long whitebaits.*

MALAWI INFORMATION DEPARTMENT

*President Banda admiring a good corn crop.*

MALAWI INFORMATION DEPARTMENT

best advantage. Only a small portion of the land is good, flat, arable land; the rest is bushland, forests, or game reserves. So the people have developed good irrigation systems and put other land to use for agriculture. Yet on Malawi's land is grown enough food to feed the whole population. The country, unlike many other African countries, is self-sufficient in food; it does not have to import food from other countries. Only in bad years of drought or locusts must extra food be imported.

The main crop in Malawi is maize (corn). Other major crops are sorghum and cassava roots (grown throughout the country) and rice and sugarcane (grown only in the lowland areas). Beans are grown in smaller quantities, and common vegetables such as cabbage, carrots, and tomatoes are grown in private gardens.

The people often help each other through farm cooperatives. While one person tills the soil with a small tractor or cultivator, others clear the bush with machetes, and still others plant the seed. When the job is done, a small party is usually held to celebrate. This spirit of helping each other carries over to building a hut or a home. Neighbors provide the

MALAWI INFORMATION DEPARTMENT

*Above: Sugarcane is cut before it is sent to be made into sugar. Below: Young Pioneers fertilize and spray a rice field.*

MALAWI INFORMATION DEPARTMENT

MALAWI INFORMATION DEPARTMENT

*Left: Workers picking tea on a plantation near Mount Mlanje.*
*Below: Where the roads are bad for motor vehicles, animals are used to transport tobacco and other products from the farms to the villages.*

MALAWI INFORMATION DEPARTMENT

materials and work together to build someone's home. Afterward a big housewarming party is held.

The government offers short courses in farmer training, sometimes less than a week long. These courses help the farmers in their agricultural practices. Instructors are mostly local teachers, but some foreign teachers also help out. Simple booklets are distributed which give suggestions in improving farming and gardening, and new seed varieties are sometimes introduced. Most of the people who attend these classes are young, including teenagers.

There are a number of strictly cash crops in Malawi. Tung trees are grown for the extraction of tung oil, used in the production of turpentine and related products. Coffee and tea plantations started by early European farmers have been expanded. More and more coffee and tea are grown each year for export. Tobacco is a crop grown in Malawi that gets a good price on the world market.

## INDUSTRIES

Industries in Malawi are very much in their infancy. The use of some products grown, such as tung-oil trees, looks promising. Certain trees are grown for their valuable lumber, some of which is exported. Textiles are another very promising industry. Malawian textiles have very colorful patterns; they are worn by Malawian women and are also exported. Shoe manufacture is yet another industry underway in Malawi. But these industries need to be developed before they will be very profitable.

To date, no valuable minerals have been discovered and exploited in Malawi. But since little of the country has been explored for minerals, valuable deposits may yet be found.

## EMPLOYMENT PROBLEMS

The number of jobs available in Malawi is not enough to satisfy all the workers. Thus, each year as many as 270,000 men migrate to the neighboring countries of Rhodesia, South Africa, Zambia, and Mozambique to find work. These men work largely in gold or diamond mines, or on large estates. It is estimated that one-fourth of Malawi's male population is employed outside the country. This is a major problem, for the government would like all of its people to be able to work in Malawi. Yet at present this is impossible, for there are simply not enough jobs. The government hopes that with training and schooling, and with the development of industry, it will be able to offer more Malawians jobs at home.

## TOURISM

Although Malawi is a small country, it is nevertheless a very beautiful one. The setting of large Lake Malawi, the many beaches and coves, the land rising up into the highlands, and Mount Mlanje in the southeast all add to the country's attractiveness. It is because of this beauty

MALAWI INFORMATION DEPARTMENT

*Above: This textile factory uses cotton grown in Malawi. Below: Shoe manufacturing is a new industry.*

MALAWI INFORMATION DEPARTMENT

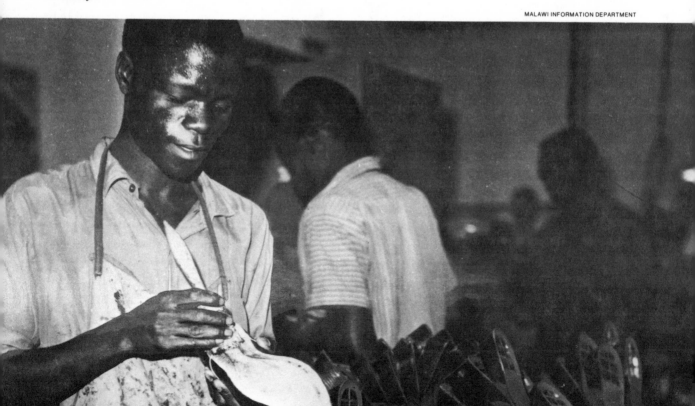

MALAWI INFORMATION DEPARTMENT

*Accommodations for tourists on Lake Malawi.*

that settlers were drawn into the region and developed settlements and towns.

Because the country is so small, Malawi cannot afford to set aside large areas to be used as game parks. But even so, the country has set aside a good deal of space for its three game reserves. These parks provide the tourist with nice accommodations and roads. But primarily they provide guides and a way to see Malawi's interesting game, birds, and flowers. The idyllic settings away from commercialized travel make this a tourist haven. With its friendly people, magnificent lake, unique mountain scenery, lush vegetation, and pleasant climate, Malawi is a natural vacation spot.

# The Enchantment of Malawi

## BLANTYRE-LIMBE

Located in the Southern Region, Blantyre is the largest city in Malawi. It is a busy city, for it is the country's business center. Contrasts between modern and traditional is quite apparent, for the streets are crowded with urban Malawians dressed in modern clothing and rural people dressed in traditional garb. Large, modern stores full of imported goods and small, open-air shops compete for customers. In front of the shops, traders sit near piles of produce or such curios as face masks, basketry, and ivory or wood carvings.

Blantyre and its suburb, Limbe, are linked by the five-mile-long Kamuzu Highway. A huge arch spans the road, from which Malawi's flag flies. The arch commemorates Malawi's independence from Britain.

Between the two cities is a rapidly growing industrial center. And nearby is a modern complex of government offices, courts, the broadcasting station, and Kamuzu Stadium. This stadium is the stage for the country's sports events and also the Republic Day celebrations.

## MOUNT MLANJE

Southeast of Blantyre is tea country. Emerald-green tea plantations stretch over the land, dotted with estates. In the distance stands Mount Mlanje, Malawi's highest peak.

Sometimes enveloped in mist and

*Victoria Avenue in downtown Blantyre is the commercial center of Malawi.*

MALAWI INFORMATION DEPARTMENT

MALAWI LAND OF PROMISE

*Above: An expressway links Blantyre and Lilongwe. Below: A new housing development in Blantyre.*

MALAWI INFORMATION DEPARTMENT

MALAWI INFORMATION DEPARTMENT

*Mount Mlanje rises 10,000 feet, the highest in Central Africa.*

UNITED NATIONS

*Fishermen pulling in a seine net along the Shire River near Lake Malawi.*

clouds, Mount Mlanje is covered by forests of mahogany, yellowwood, giant lobelias, and erica, as well as the mlanje cedar.

Nearby is Mwalawanthunzi ("rock of shade"), an ancient rain shrine. According to legend, if a traveler makes an offering to the rock, clouds will form over the rock to provide shade.

The Mwalawolemba Rock Shelter contains a number of very old rock paintings drawn more than five hundred years ago. These unusual paintings or writings are made up of circles, dots, loops, and other marks. Although the meaning of these paintings is not known, similar ones exist in other parts of Malawi, as well as in Mozambique and Zambia.

## SHIRE RIVER

On the plain southwest of Blantyre, the Shire River curves like a snake. Far in the distance are the purple mountains of the Kirk Range.

The major crossing point of the river in prehistoric times was probably at what is now called Kamuzu Bridge. This is also the site of Dr. David Livingstone's camp during his Zambezi Expedition. Below the bridge are steep cliffs. To the south for sixty miles are swamps and marshland

UNITED NATIONS

The Shire River curves through the southwestern part of Malawi.

MALAWI INFORMATION DEPARTMENT

*The 170-mile Zomba/Lilongwe Road connects the former capital with the present capital. Above: Construction of the highway. Below: The completed highway.*

MALAWI INFORMATION DEPARTMENT

MALAWI INFORMATION DEPARTMENT

*The Parliament Building in Zomba.*

known as the Elephant Marshes. For forty miles to the north are dangerous cataracts—a series of waterfalls and rapids. This rushing water was the natural barrier that prevented explorers from continuing upriver.

## ZOMBA PLATEAU

Northeast of Blantyre is the Zomba Plateau. A narrow, winding road weaves through this mountainous plateau. The road passes through thick green forests of umbrella trees, mosses, ferns, creepers, and wild flowers. Bushbuck, wild pigs, baboons, otters, leopards, and many birds abound in the forests. Among the trees on the lower slopes is the town of Zomba.

Zomba was the capital of Malawi since 1891. In the 1970s, Lilongwe became the capital and Zomba the university town. The University of Malawi is located in Zomba, as well as the State House (the president's official residence), the Parliament Building, and the Secretariat (which houses government offices).

## NEAR LAKE MALAWI

To the east, on the banks of the Shire River, is Mangoche. It was the site of Fort Johnston, one of the early British settlements in Malawi. Since Mangoche is near the southern end of Lake Malawi, both land and water birds congregate nearby. In fact, more than 240 kinds of birds have been recorded there.

At the edge of the town are acres of palm trees. From the palm leaves and rafia grasses, the local people make decorative grass mats, baskets, and even cane chairs.

North of Mangoche, on Lake Malawi, is Monkey Bay. The entrance to the bay is guarded by an island, and the bay is surrounded by many hills. Thus, the bay is protected, and its waters are very calm. For the sport enthusiast, it is an ideal spot year round. At the port of Monkey Bay, the boat *Ilala II* puts in once a week for passengers and cargo for its six-hundred-mile trip around the lake.

## LILONGWE

In the Central Region, in the midst of the Lilongwe Plain, is the city of Lilongwe. It is the headquarters for one of the largest farming areas in the country. Centrally located in Malawi, Lilongwe is at the junction of roads coming from Mozambique, Zambia, and Rhodesia. Nearby is Kasungu National Park.

The third-largest city in the nation,

*Aerial view of the capital, Lilongwe.*

MALAWI INFORMATION DEPARTMENT

MALAWI INFORMATION DEPARTMENT

*The* Ilala II *calls at Monkey Bay, where it was constructed.*

*Right: A pulpwood plantation in the Vipya Plateau region. Some trees are grown for their valuable lumber which is exported. Below: A forest nursery on the Nyika Plateau.*

MALAWI INFORMATION DEPARTMENT

MALAWI INFORMATION DEPARTMENT

UNITED NATIONS

*Much new construction has been undertaken in Malawi. Above: A one-family house is being built. Below: The new six-story Mount Soche Hotel in Blantyre.*

MALAWI INFORMATION DEPARTMENT

MALAWI INFORMATION DEPARTMENT

*A peaceful fishing scene.*

Lilongwe is now also the capital. A modern complex called Capital Hill is being constructed. It will include housing estates, parks, highways, bicycle tracks, a lake, and a business center.

## NKOTA KOTA

To the east, on Lake Malawi, is the town of Nkota Kota, originally one of the main slave depots on Lake Malawi. Nkota Kota is the largest traditional African town in Central Africa. A large Muslim mosque (place of worship) stands out in Nkota Kota, and the town is the center of Muslim activity in Malawi.

Nkota Kota is an important town historinatly for Malawians. Nor it was here in 1960 that Dr. Hastings Kamuzu Banda held his first major political rally after being released from prison.

## THE NORTHERN REGION

In the Northern Region, the road rises and falls across the Vipya Plateau, which ranges from five to seven thousand feet. Heavy forest is broken up by rolling grassland, where antelope are often seen. The hillsides are dotted with Ngoni cattle kraals (enclosures) and brightly colored wild flowers.

North of Livingstonia, the road becomes narrow and rocky over an eight-mile-long mountain pass known as the Gorode. On the steep sides are thick forests and scenic views to the valley two thousand feet below. There are waterfalls, where rivers plunge down hundreds of feet.

Karonga is the northernmost port. Originally it was a Ngonde village near Mlozi's famous slave stockade. Numerous wars over slavery took place at Karonga in the nineteenth century.

In the far north is the Nyika Plateau, with its rolling hills, golden grass, and colorful wild flowers. Scattered peaks rise to eight thousand feet. Nyika National Park covers most of the plateau.

Thus, Malawi is a blend of the traditional and the modern. Small, peaceful fishing villages still exist, while modern complexes are being built in the cities. Relics of the slave days as well as those of independence are kept as reminders of the nation's past. The people have not forgotten their long struggle for independence. But now their primary goal is to develop the country, educate the people, and turn Malawi into a self-sufficient country.

# Handy Reference Section

## INSTANT FACTS

*Political:*

Official Name—Republic of Malawi

Capital—Lilongwe

Official Languages—Chichewa and English

Literacy Rate—6-8 percent of people over 21

Monetary Units—1 Kwacha = 100 Tambala (1 Kwacha = $1.15 U.S.)

National Flag—Three horizontal stripes (top to bottom: black, red, green) with half a red sun in center of black stripe.

*Geographical:*

Area—45,747 square miles

Greatest Length (north to south)—560 miles

Greatest Width (east to west)—160 miles (including lake area)

Highest Point—Mount Mlanje (10,000 feet)

Lowest Point—200 feet above sea level (depth of lake is about 750 feet *below* sea level)

## POPULATION

Total Population—approximately 5,000,000

Average Population Density—138 people per square mile

Population Growth Rate—3 percent

Birth Rate—48 per 1000

Death Rate—21 per 1000

*Population of Principal Cities:*

| | |
|---|---|
| Blantyre | 200,000 |
| Lilongwe | 74,000 |
| Zomba | 22,000 |
| Mzuzu | 11,380 |

Population of Regions:

| Region | Population | Density (people per square mile) | Capital City |
|--------|-----------|------------------|--------------|
| Southern | 2,290,000 | 169 | Blantyre |
| Central | 1,650,000 | 108 | Lilongwe |
| Northern | 560,000 | 48 | Mzuzu |

## PUBLIC HOLIDAYS

| January 1 | New Year's Day |
|-----------|----------------|
| March 3 | Martyr's Day |
| March-April (4 days) | Easter Holiday (moveable) |
| May 14 | Kamuzu Day |
| July 6 | Republic Day |
| August (first Monday) | August or Bank Holiday |
| October 18 | Mother's Day |
| December 25 | Christmas Day |
| December 26 | Boxing Day |

## CHICHEWA WORDS AND PHRASES

| *moni* | greetings; hello |
|--------|------------------|
| *Muli bwanji?* | How are you? |
| *ndili bwino* | I'm well |
| *zikomo* | thank you; excuse me |
| *chabwino* | good; fine; O.K. |
| *pitani bwino* | good-bye (go well) |
| *tsalani bwino* | good-bye (stay well) |
| *eee!* | (expression of surprise) |
| *chonde* | please |
| *Bambo* | father (polite form) |
| *Amai* | mother (polite form) |
| *nzeru* | knowledge |
| *nbatata* | potatoes |
| *zipatso* | fruit |
| *madzi* | water |
| *mkaka* | milk |
| *ndili ndi njala* | I'm hungry |
| *ndili ndi ludzu* | I'm thirsty |
| *inde* | yes |
| *iai* | no |
| *ndifuna* | I want |
| *sindifuna* | I don't want |
| *nyama* | meat |
| *nsomba* | fish |
| *mandanda* | eggs |
| *mtengo* | price |

## YOU HAVE A DATE WITH HISTORY

200—Bantu-speaking people settle in Malawi

1000—Chewa and Nyanja immigrate to Malawi from Congo

by 1400—series of Chewa-dominated states created in southern Malawi

c. 1400—ivory trade reaches Malawi via Zambezi River; Malawi Confederation formed under "Kalonga"

by 1600—Maravi empire created

1750s—Yao ivory traders enter Malawi; Maravi empire declines

c. 1800—Ivory trade reaches north Malawi; Tumbuka kingdom prospers

1850s—Ngoni invasion takes place; Tumbuka and Chewa states disrupted; slave raids take place in southern Malawi

1858—David Livingstone and John Kirk

begin expedition up Zambezi River

1859—Livingstone reaches Lake Nyasa (present-day Lake Malawi)

1873—Church of Scotland established missions as memorial to Livingstone

1891—Malawi becomes part of British Central Africa (May 14)

1907—Formation of Nyasaland Protectorate

1915—Chilembwe rebellion takes place

1944—Nyasaland African Congress founded

1953—Formation of Federation of Rhodesia and Nyasaland

1957—Nyasaland African National Congress elects Dr. Hastings Kamuzu Banda as leader

1959—Dr. Banda arrested and jailed, state of emergency declared, fifty Africans killed

1960—Dr. Banda released, flies to London to negotiate

1964—Malawi becomes sovereign, independent state

1966—Malawi becomes republic within British Commonwealth of Nations

1971—Dr. Banda elected as life president; visits South Africa

# Index

## About the Authors

With the publication of his first book for school use when he was twenty, **Allan Carpenter** began a career as an author that has spanned more than 135 books—with more still to be published in the Enchantment of Africa series for Childrens Press. After teaching in the public schools of Des Moines, Mr. Carpenter began his career as an educational publisher at the age of twenty-one when he founded the magazine *Teachers Digest*. In the field of educational periodicals, he was responsible for many innovations. During his many years in publishing, he has perfected a highly organized approach to handling large volumes of factual material: after extensive traveling and having collected all possible materials, he systematically reviews and organizes everything. From his apartment high in Chicago's John Hancock Building, Allan recalls: "My collection and assimilation of materials on the states and countries began before the publication of my first book." Allan is the founder of Carpenter Publishing House and of Infordata International, Inc., publishers of *Issues in Education* and *Index to U.S. Government Periodicals*. When he is not writing or traveling, his principal avocation is music. He has been the principal bassist of many symphonies, and he managed the country's leading non-professional symphony for twenty-five years.

Co-author **James W. Hughes** has traveled extensively through over half of the nations of Africa and lived and worked in Kenya for several years. Dr. Hughes has contributed to journals and books in both Africa and the United States. He has served as chairman of the International Activities Committee of the National Council for the Social Studies, and has served as an educational consultant for the International Relations Committee of the National Education Association in both Kenya and Nepal. Dr. Hughes is currently Director of Teacher Education at Oakland University.